A SHEPHERD'S FRAUD: THE SLOW FADE FROM TRUTH TO ERROR

By Nicole Turner

The author assumes full responsibility for the accuracy of all facts and quotations as cited in this book.

ISBN 978-0-557-34598-4

Published by

MT Ministries Soulutions
Kansas City, Missouri * Mesquite, Texas

DEDICATION:

In memory of my mother who taught me to love the Word of God. She sleeps until "He whose right it is" returns and calls her name. And to Jay who told me to go home.

FOREWORD

Through the process of writing this book I experienced many different emotions and experiences. I procrastinated for a long time allowing different individuals' opinions on whether I should write to excuse my delay in starting. God would not let my mind rest on the issue, though, impressing on me that the book should be written. I delayed even longer worrying on what name I should choose to hide the identity of some of the individuals in the book, only to have God ask me how long I would hold off doing what He had instructed me to do.

When I finally gave in and began to write I would experience writer's block, unable to accurately make my point in an unobtrusive manner. It was during these times that I would pray and ask God's guidance on how and what to write. Inevitably on time, He would lead me to a text or quote that would state in His words first, not my own, the point I was trying to convey. Other times I would write out a thought or conclusion and, after further study or a revealed fact that God would lead me to in scripture, have to re-think my conclusion, scrap it, and rewrite a whole passage based on what God had revealed.

In the midst of everything, I had to deal with the anger I felt toward this man I had never met who has caused so much confusion and harm amongst God's people. At the same time, I was humbled because we have all been tempted to raise our ideas above God's and then try to justify it.

Refuting a system of belief is a process that is delicate, but necessary. While the goal is not to estrange those who believe what you are refuting, error must be called by its right name. I do pray that my testimony and research are presented in a way that does not offend, but instead provides the facts necessary for those who are currently in the situation I was to make an informed decision about whether to accept or reject Victor Houteff's message.

I pray that God blesses you as you read the words of this book. Some names have been changed to shield the identity of individuals referred to in the book.

From that which the Lord has been pleased to show me, there will arise just such ones all along, and many more of them, claiming to have "new light," which is a side issue, an entering wedge. The widening will increase until there is a breach made between those who accept these views, and those who believe the third angel's message. Just as soon as these new ideas are accepted, then there will be a drawing away from those whom God has used in His work, for the mind begins to doubt and withdraw from the leaders because God has laid them aside and chosen "more humble" men to do His work. This is the only interpretation they can give to this matter, as the leaders do not see this important "light."--{9MR 27.2}

"....Of your own selves shall men arise, speaking perverse things, to draw away disciples after them" (Acts 20:30). It is Satan's object now to get up new theories to divert the mind from the true work and genuine message for this time. He stirs up minds to give false interpretation of Scripture, a spurious loud cry, that the real message may not have its effect when it does come. This is one of the greatest evidences that the loud cry will soon be heard and the earth will be lightened with the glory of God.--Letter 20-1884, p. 2.

How then comfort ye me in vain, seeing in your answers there remaineth falsehood? Job 21;34

Chapter 1

Peace. It is something we desire, but we truly don't expect to have for any length of time. We are unaccustomed to lives filled with peace and are, for the most part, ignorant of the fact that it is a gift God wishes to give us. The word peace occurs 429 times in the King James Version of the scriptures[1] in 400 different verses. Two of my favorites are: "Peace I leave with you, my peace I give unto you: not as the world giveth, give I unto you. Let not your heart be troubled, neither let it be afraid," John 14:27, and "And the peace of God, which passeth all understanding, shall keep your hearts and minds through Christ Jesus," Philippians 4:7.

In the fall of 2008 I was at a point in my life where peace was a desire, but not a reality. I had just started working on my Bachelors degree and came home late one night from class to find a summons on my front door. The bank had started foreclosure proceedings on the house I rented, and my landlord informed me they would not be trying to save the house. Just a week later, I lost my job, and without that income, I began to struggle to pay my bills and one by one my utilities were turned off. The one bright spot that shined in the darkness seemed to be a new relationship with a young man named Saul[2].

We had met through a popular Adventist singles website and had begun to talk frequently through e-mail. His profile had caught my interest because it drew on my desire for a Godly mate. Our conversations characteristically held a spiritual and religious theme and our relationship was the one thing that remained consistent when everything around me seemed to be falling apart. I longed so much for peace from the storm my life had entered and he seemed to be everything my heart desired. Thus it made it very easy for me to ignore some of the indications God was placing in front of me to show me this relationship was not a wise one.

The first indications were the long and late night conversations. It was not uncommon that our conversations would last 4-6 hours at a time, the longest lasting 8 hours. This was something that excited me, because we got along so well and our conversation never seemed to dry up. It was easy to excuse the late hours in which our conversations took place because when we first switched from e-mailing each other to phone conversations I was working at night. His shift at work ended right before mine began so our conversations took up the hours that I usually filled with other mundane duties designed to keep me awake and alert. He, I easily convinced myself, was not only keeping me awake, but providing conversation that challenged me spiritually and helped my faith to grow.

When I lost my job this excuse didn't fit anymore because I needed to re-establish my natural sleeping habits. His hours, however, did not change and when he called, I answered.

What I failed to recognize was that my lack of sleep was affecting my ability to discern the accuracy of the information he was sharing with me. That, along with the emotional connection developing, made it difficult for me to diligently and consistently guard the avenues of my soul. I was not zealously protecting my mind so that falsehoods could easily be distinguished from truth.

My attention became so focused on my interaction with him that I began to neglect my daughter's need for quality time. She would come needing my attention in some matter and I would more often than not shoo her away before she had a chance to make her request known.

Exodus 20:3 says, "Thou shalt have no other gods before me", and the time and focus I was putting on Saul was very much violating this commandment. Again, I was able to excuse it because our conversations were, in my opinion, chaste, innocent, and God-focused. I reasoned that in this case it was safe to lay aside caution.

Ellen G. White cautions in *Adventist Home page 56*, "Satan knows just what elements he has to deal with, and he displays his infernal wisdom in various devices to entrap souls to their ruin. He watches every step that is taken, and makes many suggestions, and often these suggestions are followed rather than the counsel of God's word. This finely woven, dangerous net is skillfully prepared to entangle the young and unwary. It may often be disguised under a covering of light; but those who become its victims pierce themselves through with many sorrows. As the result, we see wrecks of humanity everywhere." I blinded myself to the reality of my situation because of my desire to be with Saul and by doing so opened myself up to the snares Satan had ready.

The second indication was the speed of the relationship. We had met in mid-June, early July, and while our interaction remained fairly even paced while on-line, our contact was frequent. I was, at first, very diligent to ensure that my steps were slow and carefully taken. My mistake however is that I did not as diligently seek God's approval before taking the steps in the first place. My reasoning was that, because our conversations were Godly and we got along well, our course must have God's approval.

Once our communication switched to speaking on the phone, things sped up considerably. While I have always more easily expressed myself on paper than in word, the expected awkwardness of a phone conversations did not occur and as time continued our conversations would stray from spiritual themes.

He seemed to know me in ways that were uncanny, but endearing. At times he would take the words right out of my mouth and other times he could tell me what I was doing when I fell silent on the phone. There were a few occasions where we had similar dreams at the same time of night. Had I been thinking straight, I would have recognized the enemy's stamp on these coincidences, but I let my feelings effect my perception of things and very easily allowed Satan to string me along. These things, instead of causing me to take pause, made me even more enamored and less cautious as the relationship progressed. I convinced myself quite easily that he was the man God had for me.

I had not realized it, but Saul had started to introduce pieces of the Shepherd's Rod message to me, though not by name.

Because of this I was not able to pair what he was saying with the experiences I had in the past with believers in this message.

I was not unfamiliar with the movement behind the Shepherd's Rod message, but it had never come to me without an air of negativity prior to this. It had been presented as a group of people with strange beliefs that had left the Adventist church, but continued to interact with the members in order to pull away "weak ones" into their "new light" theories. My most prominent memory of an encounter with any information related to the Shepherd's Rod movement was soon after I had given birth to my daughter. She was born out of wedlock and, because of safety concerns regarding her biological father, my address had been unlisted and made available to very few people all of which were either family or church members.

Despite this, I received a Shepherd's Rod publication unsolicited in the mail and promptly threw it away. Receiving it scared me, not because of its content, but because no one I knew had interest in the Shepherd's Rod movement, definitely no one whom I was aware had access to my address and this piece of literature had appeared out of nowhere. I was upset and all subsequent items I received went straight to the trash can until I moved. I was completely turned off also by the clandestine way they seemed to operate. Nothing clearly stated who they were and what their mission was, nor was there anything that indicated how they had acquired my contact information. Satan, though, is persistent and knew how to re-introduce it with the least resistance.

My siblings and I were raised with an intimate knowledge of the Bible. In my youth, I spent much of my spare time reading the scriptures and I always had my Bible with me (the latter habit is one I still practice today). For a short time I even desired to become a pastor, but at the time women pastors were unheard of and I was discouraged from that goal. I have always enjoyed a good scriptural discussion and this was an allure in Saul and my relationship. However, in my adulthood my childhood habit had waned and I didn't spend as much time in the Word as before, so my ability to counter the arguments Saul presented was reduced.

Initially, what he shared with me had a ring of truth to it, but I did attempt to be cautious. However, my desire to be with him made it easy for me to second guess myself and rely less on what God had shown me to be true when I was a child. He eventually identified his beliefs by their name right before I was to meet him face to face for the first time, but by then I was smitten. As I grew to care for him more, my heart desired to share his belief and I cast aside my doubts and concerns to outwardly embrace what I inwardly struggled with. I began to push away all conflicting thoughts or questions that sprang up and eventually quieted, for the most part, the voices that were calling out in warning. I felt, as I was successful doing this, that I had a clearer understanding of what God wanted me to do and I manufactured the peace I had been searching for in the beginning.

I convinced myself that this relationship was God's design and because I had done this, even He wasn't successfully getting through to me. In hind sight, it is very scary to realize that when you thought you were the closest to God you were actually quite willingly walking down the path Satan had prepared for you. Sometimes the road that leads to destruction seems to us to be the Straight and Narrow because we have tunnel vision.

By November of that year I had solidified plans to move myself, my child, and all our belongings from Missouri down to live with him in Tennessee where we would get married and live the life I had always wished for, all the while proclaiming the "new truth" of the Shepherd's Rod message to any and all who would listen. It was God's plan after all, and all the signs I wanted pointed to the confirmation of this. I was so sure, in fact, that the many voices of caution saddened me rather than alerted me as I moved forward with what I insisted was God's will.

I never convinced anyone else that it was His will, not even truly myself, but in wise love they stepped back from a battle they could not win and with their prayers of intercession gave all power to God to fight the battle for them. My mother, in particular, claiming Isaiah 49:25.

Saul's reaction, when I shared the words of caution, should also have served as a warning. He gave them little credit because he already disapproved of how those who cautioned me practiced their Christianity. He saw, and then I began to see, their words of caution and repeated approaches to reason with me as interference. I thought, "They cannot see that this is God's will!" So we…I, did not put stock into their opinions. I did feel uncomfortable with his judgmental attitude, but I had begun to doubt my ability to truly distinguish between what God approved of and what He didn't so I viewed my discomfort with his behavior as my human nature rebelling. I had convinced myself that this must be a better way. I gave myself very little credit in the long run and eventually recognized that what I thought had been me squelching my thoughts was me squelching God's voice.

Even in our chosen ignorance God works to win us to Him, because He is not willing that any of us should be lost. He is long suffering toward us and knows what is necessary to bring us back to His perfect light. He knew that my initial ignorance to the source of the message Saul shared with me would ultimately, if I took my focus off of Saul and put it back on Him, lead me to the realization of their fallacy.

I've been told that those who believe the Shepherd's Rod message tend to prey on the weaker members of the congregation who do not have a strong faith in order to more effectively woo them to their way of thinking. While this may at times be the case, my experience has been more to the effect that, intentional or not, the focus is on those who are new believers, questioning believers, or those who have experienced a great tragedy or change in their lives. That great tragedy or change can be anything from losing a loved one to death, re-entering the church after a long absence, or having a situation occur that is traditionally something the church would need to discipline.

The common denominator is not so much the weakness of faith, but rather the re-examination of views of God. It is during these times that it can be a little easier to introduce new concepts and unfortunately, false teachings. We search for better understanding when we experience situations that challenge our concept of God. That is why it is so important for the church to circle around its hurting members and love them and attend to their needs as Christ did, so that they have a stable platform to rest on and are not so easily drawn in by a friendly face that contains a wolf in sheep's clothing.

I was in that place in my life, but I had already coasted past the caution cones and was in open water with a bleeding wound and no life guard in my tunnel vision.

Many opportunities are handed over to those who would introduce falsehoods to the people of God simply by church members not approaching visitors and inviting them to dinner or offering potluck after service. When I was much younger church was an all day affair. We came to Sabbath School, moved on to Divine Worship, had potluck, and then ended the Sabbath together at AY. With these activities there were many ears and opportunities for conversation and also the ability to catch and counter false teachings that would otherwise have been shared without that benefit in the privacy of one's home.

The habit of many who hold the Shepherd's Rod message as truth to recruit more believers is to simply approach an individual after church and invite them to dinner and Bible study. No alarm is sounded because this request doesn't seem out of place. Then when they are in that individual's home, beliefs are introduced without the benefit of a countering opinion and a seed of falsehood is planted that can be difficult to uproot.

If the Shepherd's Rod message is presented in the "right" way, it is not extremely difficult to embrace at first. Truths are sprinkled generously amongst the falsehoods so that a type of logic can be followed. Eventually, though, there comes a point where one has to make some leaps to form conclusions that don't seem quite right when held up to the pure light of scripture. And though the Rod's author, Victor Houteff, claims Ellen G. White's writings support the Shepherd's Rod message one hundred percent saying, "both the Bible and Sister White's writing support the Rod one hundred percent." - *The Symbolic Code, Volume 7, Nos, 7.12 (July-*

December, 1941), p.5., it conflicts her not only on big things, but also on very basic things.

When I got to the "leaping" point I was already living with Saul and had encountered things outside of the Shepherd's Rod message that had me wondering what I had done. I was not sleeping well because I was in a situation that I knew did not honor God in that it starkly gave the appearance of and, in some cases, actuality of evil. I felt an incredible separation from God because I knew I came before Him daily impure, yet I was asking for clarification in a life or death issue: my daughter's and my salvation. I was filled with guilt because I was clearly living in circumstances contrary to His will and could not truly hear God speaking to me. Still, I sought to rationalize and excuse them. There is a time I remember kneeling in prayer next to Saul in a condition I knew with every fiber of my being God would have been justified in striking us both dead on the spot. But Praise the Lord! He is long suffering to us-ward and knew I was struggling to find my way back to Him.

My first big problem came after I read this statement by Houteff, "The question is, Do we allow mistakes in it, or do we hold that the contents in the 'Rod' are unquestionable? This we answer as follows: Analysis proves that truth has never come at any time by the power and wisdom of men, but by the Spirit of God through instruments of His own choice. Said Jesus, 'When the Spirit of truth is come, He will guide you into ALL truth.' If we should believe the words of the Master, then we must conclude that the 'Rod' contains either ALL truth or there is NO truth in it, save the quotations of truth. Therefore, if we admit one truth revealed by the 'Rod,' then we must accept it ALL. If God has been able to guide His servants in the past into ALL truth, He is able now. Therefore, we take the position that the message in the 'Rod' is free from error in so far as the ideas put forth are concerned." *-V. T. Houteff, circular letter dated August 31, 1931.* Those who believe the Rod to contain truth agree with this statement by Houteff, but this is not wise to do.

Suppose I published these statements in a book (which, ironically, I am): In my front yard there is a tree. It is tall, has thick brown bark, and many branches. Its branches are covered in leaves and the leaves are tiny spaceships.

Now, if I were to apply Houteff's theory to my statements, if one admits that my statements reveal one bit of truth, one must admit that everything revealed about the tree is true and vice versa. In this example the lack of wisdom is obvious. It can easily be proven that the tree exists, it is in my front yard, it is tall and has thick brown bark, and that it has many branches covered with leaves, but to deny the tree exists because the leaves are not tiny spaceships is just as absurd as believing the leaves are spaceships just because the tree exists.

Another problem his statement presents is that it shakes the very foundation of the Adventist faith. William Miller, the very man whose study was responsible for our understanding of what happened in 1844, came to the wrong conclusion about the event that would take place, resulting in the Great Disappointment. Our conclusion then, if using Houteff's manner of logic, should have been that we tossed out the whole teaching because it was not ALL truth and thus none of it could be.

Statements such as Houteff's are very dangerous because man often errs and misunderstands. God is the only infallible party when He is communing with man. Even Ellen G. White returned to the words she'd written down and gave clarification in areas where the understanding was not clear and God had given her greater clarity. However, the scripture quoted by Houteff is misapplied in order to prove that his writings contain truth. The reader must first assume that it is truth and then apply the verse to prove it. That is not how God works! As we see in William Miller's message, those who studied it recognized that the process was not the problem, but the conclusion, and were thus lead by the Spirit of God to realize that the event to take place in 1844 was the cleansing of the heavenly sanctuary, not the judgment of earth. Here the process was switched. They recognized that God would lead them into truth; they recognized they had the ability to be mistaken, and asked God to lead them to the proper conclusion. Houteff is so sure of himself that he takes the stand that he cannot be mistaken and so truth must be the result.

As I read the writing of Houteff and God was working with me, He led me to this passage by White that took my breath away and put into words what had been swimming around in my mind. She says,

> "My brother, you have been deceived yourself, and have deceived others. You have not searched the scriptures in the right way. You must search them to learn the mind of God, not to prove your theory. You read the Word of God in the light of your own views. You build up false structure, and then barricade it with texts which you claim prove it to be true; but you pass over those passages which prove it to be untrue. You say, 'The Bible is my foundation of faith.' But is it? I answer, the Bible does not sustain your position. Again you say, 'Show me by the Bible that I am wrong, and I will give up my views.' But how can you be convinced by the Bible as long as you wrest and misapply its utterances? By so doing you cut off the only source by which God might reach and convict you."-- *Selected Messages, Book 2, pg. 82.*

Houteff's writings are so full of false theories and weak formulas that it is useless to wade through the erroneous mixture in order to find any salvageable bits of truth, save those, as he says, that are quotations of truth.

The tree analogy is a very obvious one and easy to understand. It makes it very simple to see the absurdity. The Shepherd's Rod message, however, is not only absurd, it's deadly. I liken it to the story of Stella Nickell: a woman from Seattle who in 1988 wanted to kill her husband and make it appear to be an accident so she could collect insurance money from his death. In order to do so, she took some Excedrin capsules apart and replaced the medicine inside with cyanide. When her husband complained of a headache, she gave him the pills and he, trusting that they were what she presented them to be, took them and died. In order to ensure the cause of death was ruled an accident she randomly selected other bottles of Excedrin and did the same thing killing one other innocent person and causing another to grow very sick.

Like the tainted Excedrin capsules belied the danger within, the Shepherd's Rod message is placed in a shroud of truth. Ellen G. White and Scripture are used liberally in an attempt to deflect a cautious investigation of its claims. It is given to many in a way they trust and they ingest what they believe to be truth without perceiving the poison within. In this way it has lead and will lead to many others ingesting a lie in place of the truth. We can never know if Stella's husband suspected anything when she handed him the poisonous pills or if anything about them struck him as odd, but Houteff's statement gave me the suspicion that inspired me to examine the information I was being given and caused me to more intently study and ultimately reject the Shepherd's Rod message. It is when I did this that I was able to access the peace I had been searching for when the whole thing started.

---

[1] All scriptures come from the Authorized King James Version of Scripture

[2] Name changed

Study to shew thyself approved unto God, a workman that needeth not to be ashamed, rightly dividing the word of truth.
2 Timothy 2:15

Chapter 2

Ellen G. White states in *My Life Today pg. 107*, "In turning from God's Word to feed on the writings of uninspired men, the mind becomes dwarfed and cheapened. It is not brought into contact with deep, broad principles of eternal truth."

The term *feed* stands out to me because it gives the impression of sitting before a meal and consuming it or putting something into your body because it will do some good. She says that when this is done on the writings of uninspired men the mind becomes dwarfed and cheapened. This causes many to avoid the Shepherd's Rod message completely. However, those who believe it to contain truth use this avoidance to admonish, by quoting her statements in *Testimonies on Sabbath School Work, pg. 65*, "When a message comes in the name of the Lord to His people, no one may excuse himself from an investigation of its claims. No one can afford to stand back in an attitude of indifference and self-confidence, and say: 'I know what is truth. I am satisfied with my position. I have set my stakes, and I will not be moved away from my position, whatever may come. I will not listen to the message of this messenger; for I know that it cannot be truth.'"Sister White says no one can excuse himself from investigating the claims of a message said to be from God.

Let us be clear, though, that to feed on and to investigate are very different. Investigation gives the impression of studying something, finding what evidence is present and comparing it to facts already in evidence. An police investigator cannot go before a grand jury with haphazard evidence. The evidence must fit together in a way that when it is presented there is no room for reasonable doubt.

In the case of Houteff's writings, investigation has nothing to do with consumption. Investigation gives the opportunity to see the danger before it effects you. Feeding on the writings of uninspired men has the potential of poisoning you before you recognize the danger and then effects your ability to discern what is truth from what is error.

She goes on to say, "If a message comes…take pains that you may hear the reasons the messenger may give, comparing scripture with scripture, that you may know whether or not it is sustained by the Word of God. If you believe that the position taken has not the Word of God for their foundation, if the position you hold on the subject cannot be controverted, then produce your strong reasons; for your position will not be shaken by coming in contact with error,"--*Ibid, pg. 65*.

Investigation is crucial! In *Selected Messages, Book 2 pg. 110*, White cautions,

> "Many will honestly search the Word for Light as those in the past have searched it; and they see light in the Word. But they did not pass over the ground in their experience, when these messages of warning were first proclaimed. Not having had this experience, some do not appreciate the value of the truths that have been to us as waymarks, and that have made us as a peculiar people what we are. They do not make a right application of the Scriptures, and thus they frame theories that are not correct. It is true that they quote an abundance of Scripture, and teach much that is true; but truth is so mixed with error as to lead to wrong conclusions. Yet because they can weave Scripture into their theories, they think that they have a straight chain of truth. Many who did not have an experience in the rise of the messages, accept these erroneous theories, and are led into false paths, backward instead of forward. This is the enemy's design."

Many erroneous theories exist in Houteff's Shepherd's Rod and his subsequent publications. While I do believe that he and many of those who embrace his message meant and mean well and some may even be convinced that he spoke truth, our calling as followers of Christ is not to mean well, it is to be sure that our words and the message we set forth is congruent with God's. The Bible says in Isaiah 8:10, "To the law and to the testimony: if they speak not according to this word, it is because there is no light in them." This is how the authors of scripture agree, how the followers of God have always tested those who claim to have messages from God, and how the Adventist church in particular (along with many others) has come to view Ellen G. White as a messenger of God.

During a critical time in my study I went on a visit to my niece's school, three hours south of where I was staying. I had arranged before I left to meet with a friend in a nearby town and had shared with him that I had something to talk with him about. While there I had the opportunity to take him through what I had been studying and present some of the concerns that had started to rise. A counselor by occupation, he listened carefully to what I had to say and then at God's prompting, stressed the wisdom of me moving out of the circumstances I was in so that I could truly have a clear view of where God wanted to lead me. He also perceived my neglect of some of my daughter's needs and challenged me to refocus on my parenting and getting us both back where we needed to be. Hardheaded, I was still resistant to giving up my relationship with Saul and against the counsel he'd given, was going to send just my daughter back to Missouri to stay with family. She was just five years old at the time and one thing I did know was that I could not expose her to a belief system I was becoming increasingly unsure of myself or let her watch me continue to compromise my faith. This was yet another way God kept calling me out of my situation. Her salvation rested heavily on the way I presented God to her impressionable mind. On my way back to Saul's God used the words of my friend coupled with a series of phone conversations to fully convict me that I should not stay, but accompany my daughter.

Scripture says, "And it shall come to pass, that before they call, I will answer; and while they are yet speaking, I will hear." Isaiah 65:24. Unbeknownst to me (or him) God had sent my Pastor on a trip by car that he would normally have taken by flight. The interstate he had to take to get home placed him on a path that would allow him to meet up with us on his way home. As a result of the phone calls I had made on my journey back to Tennessee, he expected to be taking my daughter on with him, but did not know when he arrived that I had made the decision to accompany them as well. He was surprised and pleased when I informed him I was coming too, planning to follow in my car.

God tested my resolve to return home. I had been gone just two and half weeks and would be swallowing a lot of pride returning so quickly. As we left town He allowed the clutch on my car to go out. I began to think, in my fractured reasoning, that maybe He was trying to keep me there. I called Saul to see if he could suggest a good place to get the car diagnosed and during our conversation he spoke my thoughts, intimating that this could be a sign that God was trying to show me I shouldn't leave. My pastor, however, continued the work that God had begun through my friend and prayed with me. He challenged me to truly think about my situation and prayerfully make my decision. It was a hard decision because I would effectively be leaving almost everything I owned and returning home with nothing, but I did make the decision to return home. Making that decision revealed to me the difference between true peace and the manufactured peace I convinced myself I had when I headed down there more than two weeks prior.

Back at home I poured out my heart to God and pleaded with Him to forgive me for all of the ways I had maligned His name with my actions. He gave me peace in His forgiveness and with a clear conscience, I began, for the first time, to study and investigate, without outside influence, the claims of the Shepherd's Rod against the Bible and Ellen G. White.

Before I left I had told Saul that if I could truly embrace Houteff's words as truth that I would return and we would go forward with our plans. However, within a few short weeks of study, I began to see things I had chosen to overlook before and had to ultimately lay aside Houteff's writings in my quest for truth. I discovered too many troubling inconsistencies between his theories and scriptures, and, though he claimed complete agreement with them, the writings of Ellen G. White.

Near the close of my study, I sent a letter to Saul explaining why I had come to the conclusions I had. He read just the opening and, perceiving that I had chosen to reject the Shepherd's Rod, refused to read the rest. I was surprised and hurt that he would not even consider my reasoning, though I had patiently listened to his reasoning for believing it to be true. His initial reaction, though, brought back to mind a quote by Ellen G. White he had used in the past to criticize those who refused to investigate the Shepherd's Rod, "I know what is truth. I am satisfied with my position. I have set my stakes, and I will not be moved away from my position." Though he'd used it to criticize those who stood strong against Houteff's teachings, he held the position that he'd heard every argument there is against the Shepherd's Rod and refused to believe it could be false.

He had even gone so far as to criticize others who, when investigating the claims of Houteff, sought higher authority(in his opinion) to substantiate their rejection of the message, using the quote by White, "Those to whom the message of truth is spoken seldom ask, 'Is it true?' but, 'By whom is it advocated?'"--*Desire of Ages, pg. 459.*

The Scriptures, however, advise in Proverbs 24:6, "For by wise counsel thou shalt make thy war: and in multitude of counsellors there is safety." These individuals, in bringing their concerns and questions to those who had been in the faith longer and had a deeper understanding of some truths the Adventist church holds, realized that there is a spiritual battle taking place and that truth can often be mixed with a multitude of error. They sought wise counsel before they entered the spiritual battle and called to remembrance that Jesus said in Matthew 24:11, "And many false prophets shall rise, and shall deceive many," and Peter said in 2 Peter 2:1, "But there were false prophets also among the people, even as there shall be false teachers among you, who privily shall bring in damnable heresies, even denying the Lord that bought them, and bring upon themselves swift destruction," and John cautioned in 1 John 4:1, "Beloved, believe not every spirit, but try the spirits whether they are of God: because many false prophets are gone out into the world."

Eventually, Saul decided to read the whole letter, but without investigation of the points I made, rejected it. To defend his choice he used similar arguments to the ones he'd often condemned. Knowing his opinion of those who had the wisdom to search out counsel as a part of coming to their conclusions, I had approached the Lord at the beginning of my study asking Him alone to lead me to what I needed to know in order to make the right decision. I made no one else aware of what I was doing and I sought no one else's opinion on the matter. I simply opened each study session with prayer and let the Lord lead me to where I should go.

I said in my letter to Saul, "This is my letter telling you what I have found, the conclusions I have come to and my decision based on them. I realize that from our conversation today, you do not seem to feel I owe you an explanation for my decision and I do not consider this letter an explanation. However, our conversations have often included discussions concerning those who do not accept the Rod message not having real reasons for doing so or having to go to a higher authority before responding to it. I want you to know that the only higher authority I went to before writing this letter was God and the only words I am considering to come to the conclusions I have come to are those in the Scriptures and of Sister White and Brother Houteff."

When we eventually did discuss parts of my letter, he made several comments that led me to realize that he did not believe that I had sought God's guidance only. He at one time, after taking the letter to another friend to read (who also believed Houteff's writings to be true), asked which refute I had used in my letter. His question doubting the source behind my rejection of Houteff's writings only served to confirm that God had answered my prayer. Knowing how I had conducted my study and seeing that the conclusions I came to were similar enough to others who had rejected Houteff's writings as truth to make him believe I had used them instead of just my own study gave me even deeper peace, for the Scriptures say in John 16:13, "Howbeit when he, the Spirit of truth, is come, he will guide you into all truth." It became clear to me that the Spirit of Truth had unified me in thought and conclusion with those before me who had found the writings to be false, even though I was unaware of their full opinions on the matter. Truth, by its nature, brings unity and when the Spirit is leading, two who have never met can agree across spans of time on one subject. After all, this is how the scriptures flow from Genesis through Revelation in perfect harmony from one point to the next even though John never had the pleasure of meeting Moses nor Peter, Amos.

One thing that tends to be common amongst false prophets is their assurance or assertion that their words perfectly agree with scripture. Ellen G. White doesn't make a statement like this, but rather makes it clear that if we were to study the scriptures as we ought, her writings would be unnecessary. Houteff, on the other hand, stresses, to his own detriment, his opinion that his writings agree with scripture, but goes even further claiming he is also in perfect harmony with Ellen G. White. In Tract 7 of his writings, Entitled *The Great Controversy over the Shepherd's Rod*, he says, "we believe the Rod to be in perfect harmony with the writings of Sister White."

Houteff's blanket statements did a lot more damage to the Rod's influence on me than anything else. I shy away from blanket statements because they are almost always proven false. They attempt to force into harmony facts that are way too numerous to harness in that manner and cause those who connect themselves with these statements to lose credibility quickly. Because he makes no differentiation and Ellen G. White was asleep in Christ when he wrote these words, his statement must be inclusive of all she wrote.

When discussing things with Saul I would often point out where Houteff and White did, in fact, not agree. When this first happened he told me that it was not necessarily an evidence of error that their writings didn't agree, it was just that because Houteff was a more recent prophet his interpretation was more reliable than hers because his words were a "further unrolling of the scroll" or that she did not have the complete light on the subject and his writings clarified and provided new light. But Houteff's own words disagreed with this. In response to someone who had evidently made the same observation I had, he said:

> "Perhaps their grossest distortion of fact [those speaking against the Rod] is the statement: 'When the attention of the author of the Shepherd's Rod was called to this direct contradiction, he did not deny it, but claimed that his interpretation should be accepted because Sister White did not have the complete light on the subject. This allegation [that he claimed his interpretation should be accepted in lieu of EGW's] deals either in fabrication or misconstruction, for at no time have we made any such statement, neither indeed could have made it, as we believe the Rod to be in perfect harmony with the writings of Sister White." – *A Reply to the Shepherd's Rod, pg 42.*

Now this statement is very interesting because it shows that others had found where Houteff's writings and White's did not agree. But the most interesting point about this statement is what is discovered when his words here are compared to another Houteff statement recorded in another one of his publications.

Along with the Shepherds Rod, Houteff distributed various other publications one of which was called the Symbolic Code. It was presented in a format that allowed individuals to write in and ask Houteff questions about different topics. In one particular instance in *Symbolic Code, Vol. 1, No. 10, pg. 9* when someone again brought up a contradiction between his writings and White's, he answered in this way:

> Question: "5 T 212, bottom of page, seems to teach that the destroying weapons [in Ezekiel 9] are the seven last plagues. The SRod teaches that Ezek. 9 is the purification of the church. Please explain the apparent contradiction."
>
> Answer: Relative to 5 T 212, let us first observe a parallel, in certain respects, from pre-Noatic times. Jude proves that Enoch was a messenger of God, and yet that he warned his generation of the destruction of the world by the second advent of Christ when, in fact, the flood was the event which was to and subsequently did destroy the world of Enoch's time! **Enoch simply was not shown the truth of the flood**. Therefore, he preached the destruction then in terms of the coming of the Lord. So it was with Sr. White. **As no one had light** on the destruction of Ezekiel 9 she made the comparison with it to the seven last plagues with which they were more conversant.

Though he claims no one had light on the destruction of Ezekiel 9, Ellen G. White makes several comments concerning the events that take place in Ezekiel 9 and what some of the symbols represent. Peter also makes an interesting reference to Ezekiel 9, but I digress.

Despite White's numerous quotes explaining what the symbols of Ezekiel 9 stand for, Houteff gives an answer here much like the one he claims was a gross distortion of fact earlier. "*When the attention of the author of the Shepherd's Rod was called to this direct contradiction, he did not deny it, but claimed that his interpretation should be accepted because Sister White did not have the complete light on the subject.*" In the discourse recorded in the Symbolic Code he does not deny that he and White contradict each other, he just claims that no one had light on the subject. Apparently, though, he must believe he found the light because he presents his theory on the matter and expects the one who asked the question and those who read his answer to accept his interpretation.

The problem here though does not just rest with the fact that Ellen G. White gives clear information about Ezekiel 9 that does not agree with Houteff. The problem is that in trying to justify and reconcile one contradiction with White, he creates another one. He makes the statement, "Enoch simply was not shown the truth of the flood!"

This is an even more easily proven contradiction with White than is the one involving Ezekiel 9 and it is hoped that the individual who asked the question recognized this upon further investigation.

Ellen G. White says in *Spirit of Prophecy Vol. 1 pg. 6*, concerning Enoch's knowledge of the flood:

> "God communed with Enoch through His angels and gave him divine instruction. He made known to him that He would not always bear with man in his rebellion that His purpose was to destroy the sinful race by bringing a flood of waters upon the earth."

And in *Patriarchs and Prophets, pg. 85*:

> "Through holy angels, God revealed to Enoch His purpose to destroy the world by flood, and He also opened more fully to him the plan of redemption. By the Spirit of prophecy He carried him down through the generations that should live after the flood, and showed him the great events connected with the second coming of Christ and the end of the world."

And *pg. 92*:

> "Enoch had repeated to his children what God had shown him in regard to the flood, and Methuselah and his sons, who lived to hear the preaching of Noah, assisted in building the ark."

So while Houteff insists that Enoch "simply did not know the truth of the flood", Ellen G. White is quite clear that he did and not only knew, but shared that knowledge with his children, naming Methuselah and his sons (one of which was Noah's father, Lamech), who assisted Noah in the building of the ark.

When I brought these contradictions to Saul's attention, he stopped trying to prove Houteff's statements in regard to their agreement with White's and began instead to chastise me for comparing Houteff to White instead of to the Scriptures because they are to be the final word.

I agree that the Scriptures are the final word; however it seemed quite convenient for Saul's argument that Houteff was allowed to make the statement that his writings agreed with White and even use some of her writings to try and support his theories, but when I used the same process to disprove them, I was denied the privilege and chastised for doing so.

While the argument can be proven with just White's writings, White did agree with Saul in that she says, "One may come and say that he has truth, and such teachers will multiply, but we must not take their word in the matter. We must go directly to the Word. Feelings should not be our guide. The plain declaration of the Word is what is required," --*Manuscript 43, 1886.*

Reading the Scriptures did help me better understand what I was dealing with in both Saul and Houteff. The Scriptures say in James 1:8, "A double minded man is unstable in all his ways." The word double minded here in Greek is *dipsychos* which means: divided in interest. Because Saul could not show Houteff's words in this instance to be true he resorted to criticizing the way I reached my conclusion to reject the Rod. He completely ignored the validity of my argument and even continued to insist, despite the evidence from White's writings, that Enoch knew nothing of the flood.

The divided interest here is that Ellen G. White makes a statement recorded in *Selected Messages, Book 1, pg. 412* with excerpts also printed in *Testimonies to Ministers and Gospel Workers, pg. 475*. It says, "Somebody is to come in the spirit and power of Elijah, and when he appears, men may say, 'You are too earnest, you do not interpret the Scriptures in the proper way. Let me tell you how to teach your message.'" Ignoring the context of this statement within a speech that is recorded from page 406-416 in Selected Messages, Houteff's followers hone in on this one statement and believe that it is Ellen G. White prophesying of Houteff's appearance and the message he brings through the Shepherd's Rod. This is very significant, because based on the information already provided there are very basic contradictions in White's writings and Houteff's. These contradictions lead to either supporting Victor Houteff's words as truth or Ellen G. White's. If one chooses to support Houteff, it must be ignored that he contradicts White on very basic things yet still claims perfect harmony with her. It also must be considered that Ellen G. White made up the story about Enoch knowing about the flood and the angels of God speaking to him about it. If that is true, and this isn't even a portion of her writings that deals with doctrinal issues, than the rest of the information she provides for the church is highly suspect, including that portion of her speech that they believe refers to Houteff and his supposed prophetic message.

If one chooses to support White, they are left with the realization that the Shepherd's Rod is actually a shepherd's fraud, for all prophets are subject to those who come before them. It is by the prophets of old that we validate those who come after them, claiming the same calling from God.

Houteff and those who follow his teachings as truth cannot distance themselves from White when it is not convenient for them, then turn around and use White when it is. This is a divided interest and shows the double minded nature of the Shepherd's Rod message.

In *Selected Messages, Book 2, pg. 83*, Ellen G. White is also dealing with a man who believed that he had new light. It was presented to him through the visions of his daughter Anna Philips. He also used scripture and the testimonies of White to help validate the theories and claims he made regarding her visions. The admonition she gives him is appropriate also in this instance. She says, “"You have also taken from their connection portions of the testimonies which the Lord has given for the benefit of His people, and have misapplied them to the support of your erroneous theories--borrowing or stealing the light of Heaven to teach that which the testimonies have no harmony with, and have ever condemned. Thus you place both scripture and testimony in the framework of error. All who are in error do as you have done.”

Houteff makes the statement, “If the ministry can prove us wrong on the 144,000, which is the message of the hour, or even on any one topic in our publications, we agree to retract our position and destroy all of our three volumes,"--*The Warning Paradox, pg. 59.*

Proving him wrong in one topic of publication has already been done here and will be done through the remainder of this book. And it has been done in the past by those who have investigated the claims of the Shepherd's Rod message, yet, as far as I can tell this destruction has not happened. Houteff's own words are his undoing.

To the law and to the testimony: if they speak not according to this word it is because there is no light in them. Isaiah 8:20

Chapter 3

While I was living in Tennessee and on a few visits prior to moving, Sabbath afternoons were customarily spent visiting a married couple who had also embraced Houteff's writings and opened their home to invite others who were curious or interested to study with them. With the children occupied with other things he would present studies designed to tie Houteff's theories to scripture in a logical way. For the most part, Ellen G. White was not used, but I discovered during my own study that in many cases, if she had been, it would have discredited many of the theories presented. Whether this was intentional or not I do not know, but during my daily study on my own, it served to cause me to become suspicious of what was being shared.

At one such time, when it was just he, Saul and I, he shared the conclusion he had come to that it was impossible with EGW's writings alone to set up a timeline for the end times and that Houteff's writings are needed to properly understand the order of end time events. This didn't make sense to me because, prior to Victor Houteff even coming on the scene, the Adventist church had established a timeline that was used to pinpoint how events that took place in the end times lined up with each other. However, the Bible says that we are to study to show ourselves approved unto to God, and also that we are to study to make sure that what we are being told is true. Since he'd said it could not be done, I applied that test to the Spirit of Prophecy to see if what he said was true. What I found was that not only could I set up a timeline with Ellen G. White's writings, but that the timeline did not agree with Houteff's in almost any way except that Jesus was coming.

Those who believe Houteff's writings believe that during the end times there will be a pre-millennial kingdom set up on earth where the 144,000 will dwell with a great multitude they will be responsible for bringing in. This belief is based on several different theories that Houteff has established.

Probably one of the most well known beliefs, and one I mentioned earlier, held by those who believe Houteff's message is the one concerning Ezekiel 9. They believe this chapter describes what will happen to Adventists who do not embrace Houteff's teachings. His teachings are regarded by those who believe it as present truth and the acceptance of it essential to being sealed (this is connected to another belief about present truth being the seal of God). Rejecting the Shepherd's Rod leaves one open to being killed in the slaying. The slaying, it is taught, will be followed by the 144,000 going forth in the power of the Loud Cry to bring in a great multitude to the pre-millennial kingdom that Christ, at His second coming, will catch up into the air. This intertwines with the additional Houteff theory of a double close of probation, one for the Seventh-day Adventist Church and one for the rest of the world, the second of course being with those who did not come in with the great multitude. Interestingly, this belief appears similar to those who believe in the secret rapture where the sealed are mysteriously taken to heaven, while the world is thrown into turmoil resulting in more souls coming to Christ who did not heed His invitation during their first opportunity. The difference, of course, being that the 144,000, pure examples of Christianity, would be left amongst those who had yet to choose Christ.

Ellen G. White says in *Christian Experience and Teachings pg. 177* when referring to the loud cry:

> "The numbers of this company had lessened. Some had been shaken out and left by the way. The careless and indifferent, who did not join with those who prized victory and salvation enough to perseveringly plead and agonize for it, did not obtain it, and they were left behind in darkness, and their places were immediately filled by others taking hold of the truth and coming into the ranks. Evil angels still pressed around them, but could have no

power over them. I heard those clothed with the armor speak forth the truth with great power. It had effect. Many had been bound; some wives by their husbands, and some children by their parents. The honest who had been prevented from hearing the truth now eagerly laid hold upon it. All fear of their relatives was gone, and the truth alone was exalted to them. They had been hungering and thirsting for truth; it was dearer and more precious than life. I asked what had made this great change. An angel answered, 'It is the latter rain, the refreshing from the presence of the Lord, the loud cry of the third angel.' Great power was with these chosen ones. Said the angel, 'Look ye!' My attention was turned to the wicked, or unbelievers. They were all astir. The zeal and power with the people of God had aroused and enraged them. Confusion, confusion, was on every side. I saw measures taken against the company who had the light and power of God. Darkness thickened around them, yet they stood firm, approved of God, and trusting in Him. I saw them perplexed; next I heard them crying unto God earnestly. Day and night their cry ceased not: 'Thy will, O God, be done! If it can glorify Thy name, make a way of escape for Thy people! Deliver us from the heathen around about us. They have appointed us unto death; but Thine arm can bring salvation.' These are all the words which I can bring to mind. All seemed to have a deep sense of their unworthiness, and manifested entire submission to the will of God; yet like Jacob, every one, without an exception, was earnestly pleading and wrestling for deliverance. Soon after they had commenced their earnest cry, the angels, in sympathy, desired to go to their deliverance. But a tall, commanding angel suffered them not. He said: 'The will of God is not yet fulfilled. They must drink of the cup. They must be baptized with the baptism.' Soon I heard the voice of God, which shook the heavens and the earth. There was a mighty earthquake. Buildings were shaken down on every side. I then heard a triumphant shout of victory, loud, musical, and clear. I looked upon the company who, a short time before, were in such distress and bondage. Their captivity was turned. A glorious light shone upon them. How beautiful they then looked! All marks of care and weariness were gone, and health and beauty were seen in every countenance. Their enemies, the heathen around them, fell like dead men; they could not endure the light that shone upon the delivered, holy ones. This light and glory remained upon them, until Jesus was seen in the clouds of heaven, and the faithful, tried company were changed in a moment, in the twinkling of an eye, from glory to glory. And the graves were opened, and the saints came forth, clothed with immortality, crying, 'Victory over death and the grave;' and together with the living saints they were caught up to meet their Lord in the air, while rich, musical shouts of glory and victory were upon every immortal tongue."

Many Adventists believe that Shepherd's Rod believers teach that they, the 144,000, will do the slaying, but that is not true. Shepherd's Rod believers teach that it will be the five men (angels) with slaughter weapons. They validate this belief by using a misunderstood statement by Ellen G. White that the event described in Ezekiel 9 is a literal event. It is misunderstood because they apply it based on their understanding of Houteff's theory rather than based on the context in which White writes it.

In The Great Controversy 1888, pg. 656 Chapter 41, entitled *Desolation of the Earth*, White's context is very clear. Reflected not only in the chapter's title, but throughout the chapter is a clear understanding that while Ezekiel 9 is a literal event, it is the general destruction of the wicked that occurs after the final decision has been made and Christ no longer stands between the Wrath of God and the inhabitants of the earth as the mediator.

"'A noise shall come even to the ends of the earth; for the Lord hath a controversy with the nations, He will plead with all flesh; He will give them that are wicked to the sword.' Jeremiah 25:31. For six thousand years the great controversy has been in progress; the Son of God and His heavenly messengers have been in conflict with the power of the evil one, to warn, enlighten, and save the children of men. Now all have made their decisions; the wicked have fully united with Satan in his warfare against God. The time has come for God to vindicate the authority of His downtrodden law. Now the controversy is not alone with Satan, but with men. 'The Lord hath a controversy with the nations;' 'He will give them that are wicked to the sword.' The mark of deliverance has been set upon those 'that sigh and that cry for all the abominations that be done.' Now the angel of death goes forth, represented in Ezekiel's vision by the men with the slaughtering weapons, to whom the command is given: 'Slay utterly old and young, both maids, and little children, and women: but come not near any man upon whom is the mark; and begin at My sanctuary.' Says the prophet: 'They began at the ancient men which were before the house.' Ezekiel 9:1-6. The work of destruction begins among those who have professed to be the spiritual guardians of the people. The false watchmen are the first to fall. There are none to pity or to spare. Men, women, maidens, and little children perish together. 'The Lord cometh out of His place to punish the inhabitants of the earth for their iniquity: the earth also shall disclose her blood, and shall no more cover her slain.' Isaiah 26:21. 'And this shall be the plague wherewith the Lord will smite all the people that have fought against Jerusalem; Their flesh shall consume away while they stand upon their feet, and their eyes shall consume away in their holes, and their tongue shall consume away in their mouth. And it shall come to pass in that day, that a great tumult from the Lord shall be among them; and they shall lay hold everyone on the hand of his neighbor, and his hand shall rise up against the hand of his neighbor.' Zechariah 14:12, 13. In the mad

> strife of their own fierce passions, and by the awful outpouring of God's unmingled wrath, fall the wicked inhabitants of the earth--priests, rulers, and people, rich and poor, high and low. 'And the slain of the Lord shall be at that day from one end of the earth even unto the other end of the earth: they shall not be lamented, neither gathered, nor buried.' Jeremiah 25:33."

There are other particular beliefs concerning the harvest and latter rain that I hope will be explained sufficiently in the explanation that follows the chart, but I needed to point some out before the time line because not knowing would make it more difficult to understand what Houteff is saying as opposed to White.

See Figure 1 and 2 on following pages:

HOUTEFF'S TIME LINE Figure 1

The Sealing of the First Fruits	The Loud Cry	Close of Probation	2nd Coming of Christ	Millennium
Latter Rain	Outpouring of Holy Spirit	Seven Plagues		
The Ezekiel 9 Slaying/ Close of probation for Adventists (144,000 miraculously escorted to kingdom)	Sealing the of Secondfruits* (great multitude)	General Destruction of the wicked		
Latter Rain	The Harvest	Time of Trouble		
Jacob's Time of Trouble	The Invisible Coming of Christ and visible reign of anti-typical David(ensign teaching) In a pre-millennial Kingdom			

*Houteff's "secondfruits" theory will be addressed later .

SCRIPTURAL AND ELLEN G. WHITE TIMELINE Figure 2

Ezekiel 9 Sealing	Close of Probation	Ezekiel 9 Slaying	2nd Coming (The Harvest based on the words of Christ)	Millennium
Mark of the Beast		Death Decree/Sealing test		
Latter Rain		Jacob's Time of Trouble		
Loud Cry		7 Plagues		
Little Time of Trouble		Time of Trouble		

Here is how White's writings and scripture establish the End Times time line:

BEFORE THE CLOSE OF PROBATION:
The Ezekiel 9 Sealing:

> "Satan is now using every device in this sealing time to keep the minds of God's people from the present truth and to cause them to waver," *Early Writings pg 43.*

> "The living righteous will receive the seal of God prior to the close of probation," *Maranatha, pg 211.*

> "Nevertheless the foundation of God standeth sure, having this seal, The Lord knoweth them that are His. 'And let everyone that nameth the name of Christ depart from iniquity. 2 Timothy 2:19. Before the work is closed up and the sealing of God's people is finished, we shall receive the

outpouring of the Spirit of God. Angels from heaven will be in our midst," *Maranatha, pg. 212. Refer back to this quote when I address the latter rain and what it is.*

This places the sealing time now and as far back, at least, as White's lifetime. I had alluded earlier to a statement by Peter that I will share now. In 1 Peter 4:17 Peter says, "For the time is come that judgment must begin at the house of God: and if it first begin at us, what shall the end be of them that obey not the gospel of God?" So there is agreement between Peter and White in that they understood the sealing time was ongoing. The present truth then was the same as it is now. Babylon is fallen! Return to God and His infallible truths.

Houteff says, "If we were to mark out the exact time of the beginning of this sealing, we would say it began sometime during 1929."-*The Shepherd's Rod, p.32*. This is not only a contradiction, but a particularly self serving one that directly relates to when Houteff first started passing around the false message contained within the Shepherd's Rod.

Before I go through the rest of the explanation I need to point out here that believers in Houteff's message also hold the belief that the "Seal of God" is Present Truth and so one must accept the Shepherd's Rod message in order to receive the seal of God in this present time.

This is one of those areas where truth can be mixed with a multitude of error and one must be careful how they proceed. Note here that Houteff stresses that you must embrace the Shepherd's Rod message in order to receive the seal of God. In fact, if you acquire the Shepherd's Rod book from Don Adair, a Shepherd's Rod believer who leads a group in Salem, South Carolina, within the first few pages is an urge to study the Shepherd's Rod more urgently than ever. Nothing, sadly, is said of the Scriptures.

This is a key difference between Houteff and all true prophets of God. It is true that rejection of truth is a way in which many will be lost. However, all true prophets do not point to their own writings as the way in which to receive God's approval. They point to the Word of God. What must be understood here is that in every situation where a prophet was brought to God's people it was because the people had turned away from God's instructions. They were sent not to point people to what they said, but to point people back to what God said; to re-familiarize them with what God required. Going back to what God said was also the way that they were able to recognize whether a person who came with a message of God was of God. To the law and to the testimony!

Now here is where one must make sure that the path taken is dead center. Ellen G. White speaks of individuals being put to sleep in order to save them. On further investigation you can see that there were points of truth that they did not accept or did not believe were as important as others, yet because of their adherence to what they knew to be truth and their willingness to be led by God as they had been, God put them to sleep in order to save them. Why would they need to be put to sleep to save them if their acceptance of the present truth of that time was what was required of them to be saved?

The scriptures also give us examples of those who were not acquainted with the Jews who were considered God's own. Jethro was a priest of God and was instrumental in helping Moses effectively lead the children of Israel, yet he is never recorded as becoming a Jew and being required to accept the present truths that came down through Sinai by God's voice and through Moses. Neither is it said that he was condemned. Melchizedek was a priest of God and the king of Salem, but nothing more is said of him, save that Christ is after his order of priesthood, being non-Levite.

Ellen G. White gives us insight that those individuals in Sodom and Gomorrah and those peoples who were destroyed when the children of Israel entered the Promised Land had sufficient opportunity and influence to turn from their wickedness and accept God as the only one worthy of their worship. Because of the scriptures giving us insight into the fact that the Israelites were not the only people who worshipped God, we can see also that they were not the only ones who were giving an example of how to live a God led life to the inhabitants of the heathen lands. So what exactly was the present truth that they were to accept?

Another thing that must be pointed out is that the Sabbath has always been present truth. That is why the commandment says "Remember". It is the only commandment besides the fifth that does not start with "Thou shalt". For me personally, it seems to indicate that the Sabbath was not a new thing, but something they had not been adhering to. To remember something you have to have it in your mind to remember.

There have always been individuals who have kept the Sabbath as they should. The Waldenses kept the Sabbath despite the risk of their lives during the same time periods that Luther, Huss and others were being persecuted and killed. These individuals did not keep the Sabbath, yet their actions and steadfast adherence to what they knew of the truth is what saved them. It was also their willingness to point out error despite the consequences to keep the Word of God available to the world. It was their fight, their sacrifice that through God's leading allowed the Scriptures to once more be opened to common man and allow them to rediscover the old truths there in.

Even Adventists had the Sabbath truth given to them from a group of individuals already keeping the Sabbath. Within the fourth is the reason why the first three exist. This, I believe, is one of the biggest reasons that in this time where we are "rich and increased with goods" our attention must be brought back to the reason we exist which the Creator God is. It is when we reject Him and seek to focus on ourselves that we become wretched, miserable, blind, poor and naked. That is why the Sabbath is called the seal of God because it is the claim of who God is. Accepting it or rejecting it tells who we consider ourselves belonging to.

Even so, as before, Houteff's own Present Truth sealing theory and statements he makes to support it will later be shown to eliminate him from being one of those sealed and if not, discredits his message as being present truth.

The Mark of the Beast and The Seal of God:

Dignitaries in both present day and past have used a seal. The seal represents authority and when something bears a seal, it has legal ramifications. In the past it was normally used to sign documents or to approve new laws. It was, in most cases, a ring or some other inanimate object. When the king's seal was applied to something, most often with an impression into wax, it was said to bear the king's seal. In that way both the seal itself and the mark it made were referred to as the seal.

In EGW's writings she uses the term "Mark of the Beast" and "Seal of God" in the same ways. The first way is to describe what it is; the second way is to describe what it means to have the seal/mark. *"As wax takes the impression of the seal, so the soul is to take the impression of the Spirit of God and retain the image of Christ." The Faith I Live By, pg 287.*

There is no danger in concluding that if God's people are being sealed, Satan's are being marked as well. Christ says in John 10:14,"I am the good shepherd, and know my sheep, and am known of mine." A seal's purpose is to determine what belongs to whom or what is authentic when investigated.

The Mark of the Beast is placed before the close of probation and when it takes effect (the death decree/sealing test) after the close of probation based on these quotes:

"The Mark of the Beast is the papal Sabbath." *Last Day Events, pg. 224.*

> "When the test comes, it will be clearly shown what the Mark of the Beast is. It is the keeping of Sunday." *Ibid, paragraph 2.*

> "The sign, or seal, of God is revealed in the observance of the Seventh-day Sabbath, the Lord's memorial of creation...The Mark of the Beast is the opposite of this – the observance of the first day of the week." *Ibid, paragraph 3.*

Ellen G. White almost appears to contradict herself in the following quotes, but when you take into effect the reason for the seal and when the test will take place and also reread the second quote above, they help us to reconcile and better understand what she is saying:

> "No one has yet received the Mark of the Beast." *Last Day Events, pg. 224 paragraph 5.*

> "Sunday keeping is not yet the Mark of the Beast, and will not be until the decree goes forth causing men to worship this idol Sabbath. And it is not until the issue is . . . plainly set before the people, and they are brought to choose between the commandments of God and the commandments of men, that those who continue in transgression will receive "the mark of the beast." *The Faith I Live By, pg 286.*

In other words, while observance of Sabbath or Sunday will denote who has the seal, the mark is not currently affecting us because the test has not been administered. We are still in the sealing time and can decide whose seal we will ultimately bare. It is when the test is applied, and the decision is set permanently, that it is shown who has the Seal of God or the Mark of Satan. We can see the same thing in quotes relating to the Sabbath, God's seal.

> "Those who would have the seal of God in their foreheads must keep the Sabbath of the fourth commandment." *Last Day Events, pg. 220.*

> "The observance of the Lord's memorial, the Sabbath instituted in Eden, the seventh-day Sabbath, is the test of our loyalty to God." *Last Day Events, 220 paragraph 5.*

"The fourth commandment alone of all the ten contains the seal of the great Lawgiver, the Creator of the heavens and the earth." *Testimonies to the Church, Vol. 6, pg. 350.*

Latter Rain:

Victor Houteff says in his writings that the Latter/Former Rain and the Outpouring of the Holy Spirit are separate events. He bases this theory off of how he understands Joel 2 to read. However, EGW says that they are the same thing. This, of course, is a contradiction between the two. But more serious is the contradiction between Houteff and the Scriptures.
Joel 2:23, 28, & 29 reads:

> **23**: Be glad then, ye children of Zion, and rejoice in the Lord your God: for he that hath given you the former rain moderately, and he will cause to come down for you the rain, the former, and the later rain in the first month.
> **28**: And it shall come to pass afterward, that I will pour out my spirit upon all flesh; and your sons and your daughters shall prophesy, your old men shall see visions
> **29**: And also upon the servants and upon the handmaids in those days will I pour out my spirit.

Houteff takes these verses and concludes that the outpouring of the Spirit and the former/latter rain are separate events based on the word "afterward". However, in Acts 2:2-4, and 14-18, where we know the former rain is recorded, it says:

> **2**: And suddenly there came a sound from heaven as of a rushing mighty wind, and it filled all the house where they were sitting.
> **3**: And there appeared unto them cloven tongues like as of fire, and it sat upon each of them.
> **4**: And they were all filled with the Holy Ghost, and began to speak with other tongues, as the Spirit gave them utterance.

> **14**: But Peter, standing up with the eleven, lifted up his voice, and said unto them, Ye men of Judaea, and all ye that dwell at Jerusalem, be this known unto you, and hearken to my words:
> **15**: For these are not drunken, as ye suppose, seeing it is but the third hour of the day.
> **16**: But this is that which was spoken by the prophet Joel;
> **17**: And it shall come to pass in the last days, Saith God, I will pour out my spirit upon all flesh: and your daughters shall prophesy, and your young men shall see visions, and your old men shall dream dreams.
> **18**: And on my servants and on my handmaids I will pour out in those days of my spirit; and they shall prophesy.

Here Peter's wording is almost identical to Joel's when he speaks of the former rain. For scripture to be correct, and we know it is, the conclusion must be that the former rain and the outpouring of the Holy Spirit are the same thing. If the former rain is the outpouring of the Holy Spirit then the latter rain must be the outpouring of the Holy Spirit as well.

If for some reason Scripture is wrong (God forbid) then we are left to question, "When was the former rain?" Acts 2 was definitely talking about the Outpouring of the Holy Spirit. If they are not the same event where does the Bible record the former rain? If Joel 2 is interpreted the way Houteff interprets it, it had to happen before the outpouring of the spirit, for it happened that way in Joel 2.

So do we accept the Scriptures or do we accept Houteff's interpretation of scripture?

It is important to point out that here White and scripture agree that they are the same thing:

> "Let Christians…ask in faith for the promised blessing, and it will come. The outpouring of the Spirit in the days of the apostles was the former rain, and glorious was the result. But the latter rain will be more abundant." *Evangelism, pg 701.*

"We may be sure that when the Holy Spirit is poured out, those who did not receive and appreciate the early rain will not see or understand the value of the latter rain." *Last Day Events, pg 195.*

"In the East the former rain falls at the sowing time. It is necessary in order that the seed may germinate. Under the influence of the fertilizing showers, the tender shoot springs up. The latter rain, falling near the end of the season, ripens the grain, and prepares it for the sickle. The Lord employs these operations of nature to represent the work of the Holy Spirit." *The Faith I Live By, pg 334.*

"I saw the holy Sabbath is and will be, the separating wall between the true Israel of God and unbelievers' and that the Sabbath is the great question to unite the hearts of God's dear waiting saints. I saw that God had children who do not see and keep the Sabbath. They have not rejected the light upon it. And at *the commencement of the time of trouble**, we are filled with the Holy Ghost as we went forth and proclaimed the Sabbath more fully."--*Early Writings, pg 85.*

In reference to this vision EGW says:

*"'The commencement of the time of trouble', here mentioned does not refer to the time when the plagues shall begin to be poured out, but a short period just before they are poured out, while Christ is still in the sanctuary. At that time, while the work of salvation is closing, trouble will be coming to earth, and the nations will be angry, yet held in check so as not to prevent the work of the third angel. At that time the latter rain, or refreshing from the presence of the Lord, will come, to give power to the loud voice of the third angel, and prepare the saints to stand in the period

when the seven last plagues shall be poured out."--*Early Writings, pg 85.*

Knowing this is important since again White and Houteff do not agree. Here again is a point where a stand must be taken for or against White or Houteff. This is even more crucial because to believe one means the other one is in error. It is not a matter of not having light on the subject here. It's about being right or wrong. The ramifications of either affect everything else. If Ellen G. White is wrong we are again facing not being able to rely on what she says and here in an even more serious situation than that dealing with Enoch. It says that in both important and less important issues White's writings cannot be relied on and that of course influences the reliability of Houteff's based on his words. If Houteff is wrong the call is again for him to honor his vow to burn all three volumes or at least those who now hold possession of them, as he is now dead.

With scripture establishing that the Latter Rain and Outpouring of Holy Spirit as the same thing and Ellen G. White also, for the purposes of the time line, this puts the latter rain/outpouring of the Holy Spirit before the close of probation.

Loud Cry:

Houteff teaches that Christ's cleansing the temple twice represented "two gatherings, two separations, two companies – first fruits and second fruits." I'll address the "second fruits" theory a little later. This is to tie in with the belief that the first gathering is all those who claim Adventism, the first separation is the Ezekiel 9 slaying, and the first company would then be the 144,000 or those who accept the Shepherd's Rod. The second gathering would be the great multitude the 144,000 bring in, the second separation would be the separation of the great multitude from the rest of the wicked, and the second company of course would the great multitude.

White doesn't even compare the two cleansings of the temple to a people; instead she says that two cleansings represent the 2nd angel's message and the Revelation 18 angel's reiteration of the same; or two calls out of Babylon. The Revelation 18 angel's message combines with the 3rd angel's message and is termed the Loud Cry.

White says, "When Jesus began His public ministry, He cleansed the Temple from its sacrilegious profanation. Among the last acts of His ministry was the second cleansing of the Temple. So in the last work for the warning of the world, two distinct calls are made to the churches. The second angel's message is, 'Babylon is fallen, is fallen, that great city, because she made all nations drink of the wine of the wrath of her fornication' (Rev. 14:8). And in the Loud Cry of the third angel's message a voice is heard from heaven saying, 'Come out of her, my people, that ye be not partakers of her sins, and that ye receive not of her plagues. For her sins have reached unto heaven, and God hath remembered her iniquities' (Rev. 18:4,5)."*Review and Herald, Dec. 6, 1892.*The second cleansing representing the addition of the Loud Cry to the third angel's message falls into place with what Ellen G. White said concerning what takes place after God's people receive the Latter Rain. Again this is all placed before the close of probation, when the time of trouble commences.

Houteff has done in many instances what Ellen G. White cautions against in *Selected Messages, Book 2, pg. 102*, "There have been one and another who in studying their Bibles thought they discovered great light, and new theories, but these have not been correct. The Scriptures are all true, but by misapplying the Scripture men arrive at wrong conclusions...Many theories are advanced, bearing a semblance of truth, but so mingled with misinterpreted and misapplied scriptures, that they led to dangerous errors. Very well do we know how every point of truth was established[regarding the third angels message and the loud cry as well as other points of the message], and the seal set upon it by the Holy Spirit of God. And all the time voices were heard, 'Here is the truth,' 'I have the truth; follow me.' But the warnings came, 'Go not ye after them. I have not sent them, but they ran.'" Houteff has run, but God has not sent him.

Jacob's Time of Trouble and the Time of Trouble:

Houteff teaches that Jacob's Time of Trouble takes place before the close of probation. That is must take place before the 144,000 are taken into the kingdom. He also teaches that "the time of trouble such as there never was since there was a nation" will be happening while the 144, 000 are safe in the kingdom and leaving its safety only to go and bring in the great multitude.

Again, White's writings contradict this. Scripture doesn't even mention anything of the sort. She places Jacob's time of trouble after the close of probation a time when God's people stand without a mediator as Christ has left the Sanctuary. She says in *Spirit of Prophecy Vol. 4, Chapter 34, pg. 431-432*:

> "When the third message closes, mercy no longer pleads for the guilty inhabitants of earth. The people of God have accomplished their work; they have received the latter rain, or the refreshing from the presence of the Lord and they are prepared for the trying hour ***before*** them. Angels are hurrying to and fro in heaven. An angel returning from earth announces that his work is done, the seal of God has been placed upon His people. Then Jesus ceases His intercession in the sanctuary above. He lifts His hands, and with a loud voice says, 'It is done'; and all the angelic host lay of their crowns as He makes the solemn announcement: "He that is unjust, let him be unjust still; he that is filthy, let him be filthy still; and he that is righteous, let him be righteous still, and he that is holy let him be holy still.' ***Every*** case has been decided for life or death. Christ has made the atonement for his people, and blotted out their sins. The number of His subjects is made up; 'the kingdom and dominion and the greatness of the kingdom under the whole heaven is about to be given to the heirs of salvation, and Jesus is to reign as king of kings and Lord of Lords.

> When He leaves the sanctuary, darkness covers the inhabitants of the earth. In that fearful time the righteous must live in the sight of a holy God without an intercessor. The restraint which has been upon the wicked is removed, and Satan has entire control of the finally impenitent. The power attending the last warning has enraged them, and their anger is kindled against all who have received the message. The people of God are then plunged into those scenes of affliction and distress described by the prophet as the time of Jacob's Trouble." (Jer. 30: 5-7)

Here we see not only does Jacob's time of trouble take place after the close of probation, but also that EVERY case is decided. After Christ divests of His priestly robes, Michael (Christ) stands up and His people are soon delivered out of it. This is the Ezekiel 9 slaughtering time (not at all spiritual, but literal) and also what is referred to as the time of trouble when the 7 plagues are being poured out. Here we see that contrary to Houteff's theory the Ezekiel 9 slaughtering is the general destruction of the wicked, not a time reserved exclusively for those in the church who reject his message. White says,

> "Unless they repent, and leave the work of Satan in oppressing those who have the burden of the work and in holding up the hands of sinners in Zion, they will never receive the mark of God's seal of approval. They will fall in the general destruction of the wicked, represented by the work of the five men bearing slaughter weapons."
> *Testimonies for the Church, Vol. 3, pg. 267.*

Harvest:

In reference to the Matthew 13 parable concerning the harvest Houteff says, "The Harvest is the Loud Cry of the third angel's message." *SR Vol. 1, pg 104.* He also says: "The Harvest itself necessarily precedes the close of probation."

While EGW says much on this subject, I want to use the words of Christ first when explaining the same parable. In Matthew 13:38-43 Christ says,

> "He answered and said unto them, He that soweth the good seed is the Son of man; The field is the world; the good seed are the children of the kingdom; but the tares are the children of the wicked one; The enemy that sowed them is the devil; the harvest is the end of the world; and the reapers are the angels. As therefore the tares are gathered and burned in the fire; so shall it be in the end of this world. The Son of man shall send forth his angels, and they shall gather out of his kingdom all things that offend, and them which do iniquity; And shall cast them into a furnace of fire: there shall be wailing and gnashing of teeth. Then shall the righteous shine forth as the sun in the kingdom of their Father. Who hath ears to hear, let him hear.

Houteff's followers have the understanding (revealed in a study provided on Matthew 13 accessible on a prominent Shepherd's Rod website: www.shepherds-rod-message.org) that the Harvest here does not necessarily mean the Second Coming of Christ. "This does not necessarily mean Christ second coming. COL [page] 72 (Christ's Object Lessons) puts the harvest at the end of probationary time. Heb 9:24-26 puts the end of the world at the time Christ entered into the most holy place to 'put away sin by the sacrifice of himself.'" Houteff uses this at the opening of the study to establish that these two events though using the same terms use them to talk about different times so that a foundation can be made to argue that Christ referring to the harvest as the end of the world doesn't have to mean the actual end of the world. However page 72 of Christ's Object Lessons doesn't put the harvest at the end of probationary time. Page 72 says:

> "There is in the Saviour's words another lesson, a lesson of wonderful forbearance and tender love. As the

tares have their roots closely intertwined with those of the good grain, so false brethren in the church may be closely linked with true disciples. The real character of these pretended believers is not fully manifested. Were they to be separated from the church, others might be caused to stumble, who but for this would have remained steadfast.

"The teaching of this parable is illustrated in God's own dealing with men and angels. Satan is a deceiver. When he sinned in heaven, even the loyal angels did not fully discern his character. This was why God did not at once destroy Satan. Had He done so, the holy angels would not have perceived the justice and love of God. A doubt of God's goodness would have been as evil seed that would yield the bitter fruit of sin and woe. Therefore the author of evil was spared, fully to develop his character. Through long ages God has borne the anguish of beholding the work of evil, He has given the infinite Gift of Calvary, rather than leave any to be deceived by the misrepresentations of the wicked one; for the tares could not be plucked up without danger of uprooting the precious grain. And shall we not be as forbearing toward our fellow men as the Lord of heaven and earth is toward Satan?

The world has no right to doubt the truth of Christianity because there are unworthy members in the church, nor should Christians become disheartened because of these false brethren. How was it with the early church? Ananias and Sapphira joined themselves to the disciples. Simon Magus was baptized. Demas, who forsook Paul, had been counted a believer. Judas Iscariot was numbered with the apostles. The Redeemer does not want to lose one soul; His experience with Judas is recorded to show His long patience with perverse human nature; and He bids us bear with it as He has borne. He has said that false brethren will be found in the church till the close of time."

It is on pages 74 and 75 that it talks about the harvest and it puts it at Christ's second coming:

> "The tares closely resembled the wheat while the blades were green; but when the field was white for the harvest, the worthless weeds bore no likeness to the wheat that bowed under the weight of its full, ripe heads. Sinners who make a pretension of piety mingle for a time with the true followers of Christ, and the semblance of Christianity is calculated to deceive many; but in the harvest of the world there will be no likeness between good and evil. Then those who have joined the church, but who have not joined Christ, will be manifest.
>
> The tares are permitted to grow among the wheat, to have all the advantage of sun and shower; **but in the time of harvest ye shall "return, and discern between the righteous and the wicked, between him that serveth God and him that serveth Him not." Mal. 3:18**. Christ Himself will decide who are worthy to dwell with the family of heaven. He will judge every man according to his words and his works. Profession is as nothing in the scale. It is character that decides destiny.
>
> The Saviour does not point forward to a time when all the tares become wheat. **The wheat and tares grow together until the harvest, the end of the world.** Then the tares are bound in bundles to be burned, and the wheat is gathered into the garner of God. "Then shall the righteous shine forth as the sun in the kingdom of their Father." Then "the Son of man shall send forth His angels, and they shall gather out of His kingdom all things that offend, and them which do iniquity; and shall cast them into a furnace of fire; there shall be wailing and gnashing of teeth."

She says that the wheat and tares will grow together until the harvest, the end of the world. And she says at the time of harvest ye (meaning Christ) shall return and discern which places the harvest at Christ's second coming.

He teaches that Hebrews 9:24-26 puts the end of the world when Christ appeared to "put away sin by the sacrifice of himself" but the problem here is that the verse says *in* the end of the world.

> 24:For Christ is not entered into the holy places made with hands, which are the figures of the true; but into heaven itself, now to appear in the presence of God for us:
> 25: Nor yet that he should offer himself often, as the high priest entereth into the holy place every year with blood of others;
> 26: For then must he often have suffered since the foundation of the world: but now once in the end of the world hath he appeared to put away sin by the sacrifice of himself.

That he died in the end of the world is true for His sacrifice was the exclamation point on the plan of salvation. It was the sacrifice that all other sacrifices, from the beginning of the world when Adam first killed a lamb for his sins to the very sacrifice that was in the midst of happening when the curtain of the temple was torn apart from top to bottom, pointed to and was the last and only sacrifice that covered the sins of all.

Because Satan saw that he was unsuccessful in causing Jesus to fall, he immediately began to set into motion the things by which the world will end. The very prophecies by which the church stands and Daniel says will occur during the time of the end were in motion at that time, but the end of the end was "not yet".

Another way to look at it is that Christ did not put sin away when he appeared and died on our behalf. We are still dealing with sin every day. It is at His second coming that Christ will ultimately put sin away, in that it will no longer be effecting His own, those who He, at His second coming, harvests from the earth.

Thus we see that in both examples given the reference is in fact the Second Coming of Christ.

THE "SECONDFRUITS" THEORY

In earlier portions of this book you have seen the term *secondfruits* used. This is a term that Houteff made up to describe the great multitude that the 144,000 are to bring in after the Ezekiel 9 slaying of the apostate Adventists; apostate, of course, because they reject the Shepherd's Rod message, not because they have not stayed true to God's Word.

The term itself demonstrates a lack of understanding concerning the agricultural symbols used in scripture. The faulty logic behind why it was adopted further demonstrates this lack of understanding and gives an example of some of the loose logic Houteff uses to form the theories he has.

The Bible uses different symbols when describing different events. In scripture there is absolutely no reference whatsoever to secondfruits. There is however a reference to firstfruits. In every situation first fruits are used to describe a smaller representation of a greater whole. The first fruits of the harvest, those who were raised with Christ at his resurrection, and even Christ, Himself. Scriptures often utilize the Jewish economy to explain the plan of salvation and the work of the Holy Spirit. This is where we find familiarity with several agricultural terms including the latter rain, former rain, and of course, first fruits.

This is important to understand because understanding the Jewish economic system and the terms used within it helps us to understand the plan of salvation presented in scriptures on a deeper level. It also helps to point out some very serious problems with Houteff's theory of secondfruits.

Houteff's logic is reflected in this quote, "As the 144,000 are the 'firstfruits' there must be second fruits, for where there is first, there must also be second. And as the first fruits are the 'servants of God,' they must subsequently be sent to all nations to gather the second fruits (Isaiah 66:19-20)-the great multitude of

Revelation 7:9, whom John saw after viewing the sealing of the 144,000."*Behold the Lion of the Tribe of Judah, the Root of David" (1937), p.16-17.*

Now let's take a closer look. Based on Houteff's logic, one can also conclude that there are thirdfruits and fourthfruits and even fifthfruits, and on at nauseam until the end of time, or harvest depending on how you look at it, for numbers continue on through infinity as long as you add one.

The use of formulas is not unheard of in the Adventist church or in many other denominations. Formulas are used to determine prophetic times and understand other portions of scripture. However, there is a method to the formulas used and because of this method these formulas can work in different settings no matter what, for example the day = year formula. This has allowed the Adventist church to understand the 2300 day prophecy, the 1260 day prophecy and many other time related prophecies in scripture, including the half hour silence in heaven recorded in Revelation.

If we use Houteff's formula for creating the secondfruits theory, we can create a whole other doctrine for ourselves, which in fact he has. Since there was a first coming and we expect a second coming we can than create our own theory that says because of the first and second coming there must be a third coming and fourth coming and fifth coming.

But we do not believe this. Why? Most importantly, because Scripture gives no support of a third, or fourth, or fifth coming. The formula is too general to safely use in other situations and is not a formula derived from scripture, but rather from man's imagination. The most significant reason though is because there are no secondfruits in the Jewish economic system.

The firstfruits are a representation of the greater whole and are not followed by second fruits. An easy way of describing this is imagining a jar of peanut butter. When you open it for the first time and scoop the knife in, the peanut butter you pull from the jar is technically the firstfruits of your peanut butter. The peanut butter on your knife represents what is in the jar and lets you know each time you dip what you will get.

Scripture tells us that the sacrifices and the Sanctuary ceremonies represented on earth an example of what takes place in the heavenly sanctuary. Christ first is our sacrifice, then He is our High Priest, then, and most importantly, He is our reigning King and victorious Rescuer.

Ellen G. White says that it is through the Jewish economic system that we understand the plan of salvation. "The significance of the Jewish economy is not yet fully comprehended. Truths vast and profound are shadowed forth in its rites and symbols. The gospel is the key that unlocks its mysteries. Through a knowledge of the plan of redemption, its truths are opened to the understanding. Far more than we do, it is our privilege to understand these wonderful themes."--*Christ's Object Lessons, p.133*. It is the gospel that is the key, not the Shepherds Rod. So let us look at the Jewish economic system and see what it tells us with the gospel as our key.

There were seven feasts celebrated by the Jews throughout the year: Passover, Unleavened Bread, First Fruits, Weeks/Pentecost, Trumpets, Day of Atonement, and Tabernacles or booths.

During the Passover a wave sheaf of the new crop of grain was presented to God as first fruits, marking the beginning of the barley harvest. This was a requirement given by God in Leviticus 23:10, "Ye shalt bring a sheaf of the first fruits of your harvest unto the priest."This not only signified the beginning of the barley harvest, but the entire harvesting period.

Ellen G. White says in *The Desire of Ages, pg. 785*, "Christ arose from the dead as the first fruits of those that slept. He was the antitype of the wave sheaf, and His resurrection took place on the very day when the wave sheaf was to be presented before the Lord. For more than a thousand years this symbolic ceremony had been performed. From the harvest fields the first heads of ripened grain were gathered, and when the people went up to Jerusalem to the Passover the sheaf of first fruits was waved as a thank offering before the Lord. Not until this was presented could the sickle be put to the grain, and it be gathered into sheaves. The sheaf dedicated to God represented the harvest. So Christ the first fruits represented the great spiritual harvest to be gathered for the kingdom of God. His resurrection is the type and pledge of the resurrection of all the righteous dead. 'For if we believe that Jesus died and rose again, even so them also which sleep in Jesus will God bring with Him.' 1 Thessalonians 4:14." Scripture tells us in Matthew 27:52-53that when Jesus was crucified there was an earth quake and "the graves were opened; and many bodies of the saints which slept arose, and came out the graves after his resurrection, and went to the holy city, and appeared unto many." White gives further insight, saying, "During His ministry, Jesus had raised the dead to life. He had raised the son of the widow of Nain, and the ruler's daughter and Lazarus. But these were not clothed with immortality. After they were raised, they were still subject to death. But those who came forth from the grave at Christ's resurrection were raised to everlasting life. They ascended with Him as trophies of his victory over death and the grave. These, said Christ, are no longer the captives of Satan; I have redeemed them. I have brought them from the grave as the first fruits of My power, to be with Me where I am, never more to see death or experience sorrow."-*Desire of Ages, p. 785-786.*

Concerning Jesus upon his return to heaven after his resurrection, she says, "He points to the tokens of His triumph; He presents to God the wave sheaf, those raised with Him as representatives of that great multitude who shall come forth from the grave at His second coming....Christ was the first-fruits of them that slept...This very scene, the resurrection of Christ from the dead, had been celebrated in type by the Jews. When the first heads of grain ripened in the field, they were carefully gathered; and when the people went up to Jerusalem; these were presented to the Lord as a thank offering. The people waved the ripened sheaf before God, acknowledging Him as the lord of the harvest. After this ceremony the sickle could be put to the wheat, and the harvest gathered....So those who had been raised were to be presented to the universe as a pledge of the resurrection of all who believe in Christ as their personal Saviour."-*The Desire of Ages, pg. 834, The Youth's Instructor, August 11, 1898, paragraph 4, 5.*

It is important to recognize that Christ is referred to as the first fruit, but he also presents those who rose with Him to God as a wave sheaf. It is here that we see Christ stepping into His role as the High Priest. He was first our sacrifice and then our mediating high priest. The first fruit that He brought with Him are the first representatives of those who stood worthy before God only because they were covered by the blood of Christ.

Second fruits are not mentioned here because the first fruits presented by Christ to God represented the "pledge of the resurrection of all who believe in Christ as their personal Saviour." They represented "the great multitude who shall come forth from the grave at His second coming." Here the second fruits theory fails and in order to be a sound formula or theory, it should be able to apply to every situation where there is a first fruit/second fruit type scenario.

After the Passover was celebrated it was followed by the seven day Feast of Unleavened Bread and first fruits. Ellen G. White tells us, "The slain lamb, the unleavened bread, the sheaf of first fruits, represented the Saviour,"-*The Desire of Ages, pg. 77.* It was on the second day of this festival that the wave sheaf was presented to God. As read earlier, this was the very day Christ was raised from the dead and ascended unto the Father. Understanding this gives more significance to His admonition to Mary not to touch Him when she first recognized Him in the garden.

Fifty days later was the feast of Pentecost or Weeks. On that day, two loaves of bread were made from the harvested grain, this time with leaven, and were presented to God as first fruits. This process marked the end of the wheat harvest. This practice is recorded in Leviticus as well in chapter 23:17, "Ye shall bring out of your habitations two wave loaves of tenth deals; they shall be of fine flour; they shall be baken with leaven; they are the first fruits unto the Lord." Ellen G. White provides this statement about what these first fruits represent, "The Pentecost was a feast celebrated seven weeks after the Passover. Upon these occasions the Jews were required to repair to the temple and to present the firstborn of all the harvest, thus acknowledging their dependence on the great Giver of all good, and their obligation to render back to God, in gifts and offerings to sustain His cause, that which He had entrusted to them. On this day of divine appointment, the lord graciously poured out His Spirit on the little company of believers, who were the first-fruits of the Christian church," *The Spirit of Prophecy Vol. 3, pg. 265*. This "little company of believers" went on to build up the Christian church and baptize both far and wide. Many of those whom they encountered, Scripture tells us, received the Holy Spirit. Never were they called second fruit. The "little company" represented the greater whole, all which, upon hearing the gospel of Jesus Christ joined the Christian church and joined the disciples in declaring the gospel to the world. We are a part of that greater whole.

Between the Pentecost and the Feast of Tabernacles came the Day of Atonement. The Day of Atonement was the time when the High Priest went into the Most Holy Place for the purposes of cleansing the sanctuary and presenting the blood of the sacrifices to cleanse the camp of all its sin.

This is the event that, as Adventists, we believe began in 1844. We are living in the anti-typical Day of Atonement and Christ is now, as our High Priest, advocating on our behalf and using His blood to cover our sins as we cling to His righteousness as ours.

The last feast to take place in the year was the Feast of Tabernacles. "And the LORD spake unto Moses, saying, The fifteenth day of this seventh month shall be the feast of tabernacles for seven days unto the LORD." Leviticus 23:33,34. Ellen G. White says, "This feast was to be pre-eminently an occasion of rejoicing. It occurred just after the great Day of Atonement, when the assurance had been given that their iniquity should be remembered no more. At peace with God, they now came before Him to acknowledge His goodness and to praise Him for His mercy. The labors of the harvest being ended, and the toils of the new year not yet begun, the people were free from care, and could give themselves up to the sacred, joyous influences of the hour.

"The Feast of Tabernacles was the closing gathering of the year. It was God's design that at this time the people should reflect on His goodness and mercy. The whole land had been under His guidance, receiving His blessing. Day and night His watch care had continued. The sun and rain had caused the earth to produce her fruits. From the valleys and plains of Palestine the harvest had been gathered. The olive berries had been picked, and the precious oil stored in bottles. The palm had yielded her store. The purple clusters of the vine had been trodden in the wine press...The feast continued for seven days, and for its celebration the inhabitants of Palestine, with many from other lands, left their homes, and came to Jerusalem. From far and near the people came, bringing in their hands a token of rejoicing. Old and young, rich and poor, all brought some gift as a tribute of thanksgiving to Him who had crowned the year with His goodness and made His paths drop fatness."--*Desire of Ages, p.447-448.*

In this time, as we work out our own salvation with fear and trembling, we look toward this blessed feast, where we will be able to rejoice and be caught up in the sacred joy of the celebration, knowing that not just the years sins, but all our sins forever more are forgiven and never will sin rise again. Says White, "The Feast of Tabernacles was not only commemorative, but typical. It not only pointed back to the wilderness sojourn, but, as the feast of harvest, it celebrated the ingathering of the fruits of the earth, and pointed forward to the great day of final ingathering, when the Lord of the harvest shall send forth His reapers to gather the tares together in bundles for the fire, and to gather the wheat into his garner. At that time the wicked will all be destroyed.

"The people of Israel praised God at the Feast of Tabernacles, as they called to mind His mercy in their deliverance from the bondage of Egypt and his tender care for them during their pilgrim life in the wilderness. They rejoiced also in the consciousness of pardon and acceptance, through the service of the day of atonement, just ended. But when the ransomed of the Lord shall have been safely gathered into the heavenly Canaan-forever delivered from the bondage of the curse, under which 'the whole creation groaneth and travaileth in pain together until now' (Romans 8:22)-they will rejoice with joy unspeakable and full of glory. Christ's great work of atonement for men will then have been completed, and their sins will have been forever blotted out."-*Patriarchs and Prophets, pg. 541-542.*

Throughout the extensive examples represented in the sanctuary service there are many things presented, but nowhere is there even a suggestion of second fruits. It is because the term had no part in the Jewish economy and because it has no place in scriptural doctrine.

Three points need to be made here for future reference: First, the High Priest did not leave the Most Holy Place until after he was finished ministering and atoning for the sins of the camp, that included both the Israelites and those who were not Israelites, for strangers were held to the same responsibilities as the Israelites. Second, when he left the Most Holy Place, the people were assured that they had been cleansed from their sins. Third, the Feast of Tabernacles, the celebration after the Day of Atonement, took place after the harvest was complete and all that was supposed to be brought in was brought in.

Preach the word; be instant in season, out of season; reprove, rebuke, exhort with all longsuffering and doctrine. For the time will come when they will not endure sound doctrine; but after their own lusts shall they heap to themselves teachers, having itching ears; And they shall turn away their ears from the truth, and shall be turned unto fables.2 Timothy 4:2-4

Chapter 4

Since I was a little girl, I have always daydreamed about heaven. That all the wonderful things I thought up and read would pale in comparison to the reality made my giddiness all the more evident. There was little I looked forward to more than going to heaven. Meeting Jesus and enjoying the new earth pulled ahead on the list.

As I matured and grew older, I became fairly well versed, I believed, in what was going to happen when Christ returned. There were things, of course, I did not understand, but they were not enough to dim my hopes or make it unattractive.

When Saul first presented the concept of a pre-millennial kingdom I was sure that the concept was unfounded. I wasn't yet enamored with him so we agreed to disagree. The subject, however, came up again after I was and became a subject we went back and forth on. I eventually accepted the teaching, not because I was convinced it was true, but because I was not equipped to dispute it, and he wouldn't have been convinced even if I had been.

The study I was given in order to establish proof of a pre-millennial kingdom was similar to this one found on the same Shepherd's Rod website mentioned earlier, but it should be noted that on the charts Houteff created, used, and that are still used, there is no indication or mention of a pre-millennial kingdom.

Kingdom Study Figure 3

THE ESTABLISHMENT OF THE KINGDOM OF GLORY

INTRODUCTION: Most SDAs are aware of the establishment of the kingdom of glory but believe it begins with Christ 2nd advent and continues to the New Earth. Although God's kingdom of glory includes the millennium and the New Earth, the Scriptures clearly reveal that it will begin partially before the 2nd advent. The object of this study is to establish this and show how, why, and where this kingdom will be established.

1. THE OLD TESTAMENT CHURCH EXPECTED THE KINGDOM OF GLORY

1. **Isa. 9:6, 7** The Jews expected the Messiah to establish the kingdom of glory in their day. With the promise of the birth of the Messiah (Christ) also came the promise of the establishment of His kingdom.

2. THE APOSTLES EXPECTED THE KINGDOM IN THEIR DAY

1. **Acts 1:6, 7** The Lord did not say that the kingdom was not to be established, but that it was not for them to know the times or the seasons. The Jews and the Apostles had studied this promise and were expecting Christ to set up His kingdom at that time.

3. THE KINGDOM TO BE EXTABLISHED IN THE LATTER DAYS

1. **Daniel 2:44** Here we see that the Kingdom is to be established in the days of the ten-toe kings (Our present world **1T 361**). We must therefore be looking for the establishment of the kingdom not before our present world, not after our present world, but **in.--during our present world.**
2. We also note that the stone is the same as the kingdom because they both smite the image. The stone is the 144,000
3. The stone was a kingdom before it smote the image (**verse 44**) and it (the kingdom)shall destroy all these kingdoms...This proves that the kingdom is established before the finishing of the gospel.

4. GOD'S ETERNAL PURPOSE FOR ISRAEL TO BE FUFILLED WITH THE SDA CHURCH.

1. **PK 19** The people of God were to extend the borders of their kingdom to embrace the whole world. God intended that the earth was to be filled with righteousness from border to border.
2. **PK 713, 714** Even though ancient Israel did not fulfill this commission, God's word cannot return to Him void. Thus we see that what ancient Israel failed to do, it will be accomplished through the Israel of today. **PK 22, 299**
3. **Ps. 105:8-11** This verse describes what the covenant is and definitely reveals that God will remember it forever. The covenant says, unto thee will I give the land of Canaan. The kingdom established in Palestine.

5. THE KINGDOM ESTABLISHED IN THE LATTER DAYS

I. **Jer. 30:3, 4** This promise of restoration is **unconditional,** and that it includes the return of **Israel** and **Judah** (all 12 tribes) to the land of their fathers (Canaan/Palestine). This will be fulfilled in the latter days.

2. When Jeremiah was writing, only two tribes existed as a nation. The ten tribes had been scattered many years before in 721 B.C.

3. **Jer. 23:5-8** This promise also is **unconditional** and refers to all 12 tribes in the Latter days.

4. **Hosea 3:4, 5** Here we see that after many days of obscure wondering, without their own government (king or prince), and without the temple and its services (sacrifice, ephod, teraphim), all the tribes (children of Israel) will return (to the land of their fathers) and establish a kingdom.

6. WHAT WILL THE PRE-MILLENNIAL KINGDOM BE LIKE?

1. **Isa. 11:1-12** This passage could not be referring to Heaven during the millennium or to the New Earth because:

a. There will be no Gentiles to seek the kingdom

b. No such gathering described in verses 11, 12 will take place in Heaven or the New Earth.

c. There will be no births in the New Earth. Hence, there will be no children.

1SM 172, 173; Luke 20:27-36

2. Therefore Isaiah here must be speaking of a time when there will be Gentiles seeking to join God's kingdom, and a great gathering from various nations, and when sucking, weaned, and little children exist.

7. THE KINGDOM AND THE NEW HEART EXPERIENCE

1. **Ezekiel 36:16-37** Here we see that God is to cleanse His people from their sins. Hence only those who have embraced the righteousness of Christ will inherit the land. The kingdom is to be a witness to the heathen. This is the grandest object of the kingdom being established here on earth prior to the coming of our Lord.

FURTHER TEXTS OF PROOF:

1. **Zech. 8:1-8** There will be no old men and women, or little children in the New Jerusalem.

2. **Ezekiel 37:15-28** Israel and Judah have not as yet been a kingdom together

3. **Ezekiel 48:1-16** This passage describes a new and unfulfilled set-up of Palestine.

SUMMARY: We have seen that the Kingdom of God has a very small beginning. However, it is to grow and extend its borders, just as God has intended for ancient Israel. We have also found that internal conditions are to be different from those of any previous earthly kingdom, because it is based upon the reign of Christ's righteousness in the hearts of His people. It is to be a kingdom of believers.

Part of the logic used in this study is based on the previous acceptance of the theory of Houteff about Daniel 2 which we'll address a little later. The other is focused largely on the words "in the days of those kings" and what Houteff believed that to mean.

The study starts with Isaiah 9:6, 7 and Acts 1:6,7 to establish that both the old testament church and the apostles expected the kingdom to accompany the Messiah's appearance. While this is true, it must also be acknowledged that Christ made it very clear that this understanding was incorrect and that it would not take place in the way they expected. They were expecting an earthly kingdom that would re-exalt them to the position they had once held as the chosen people of God. Christ told them again and again that His kingdom was not of this world and that no one would be able to say "lo here or lo there" to find it (Luke 17:20, 21). Ellen G. White shares that even in His youth He corrected the misconceptions of those who expected His coming. Unbeknownst to them, the Messiah was sitting at their feet asking them questions designed to get them to re-examine the prophecy of His coming, focusing on those points that spoke of His suffering and death. She says, "The rabbis spoke of the wonderful elevation which the Messiah's coming would bring to the Jewish nation; but Jesus presented the prophecy of Isaiah, and asked them the meaning of those scriptures that point to the suffering and death of the Lamb of God....They could not see that their expectation in regard to the Messiah was not sustained by prophecy; but they would not renounce their theories that had flattered their ambition."--*The Desire of Ages, pg. 78-80.*

Every time I was close to being convinced, these words of Christ would bring me back to the truth.

The word *observation* used in Luke is translated from the Greek word *parateresis* which means in such a manner that it can be watched with the eyes; or in a visible manner.

Jesus used these words to explain that the visible kingdom expected was not what kingdom He was there to establish. He was there to establish the kingdom in the hearts of those who believed.

This understanding Paul shares in Colossians 1:12, 13. "Giving thanks unto the Father, which hath made us meet to be partakers of the inheritance of the saints of light: Who hath delivered us from the power of darkness, and hath translated us into the kingdom of his dear son."

He says also in 1 Corinthians 15:50 that flesh and blood cannot inherit the kingdom. The Greek words used here *sarx* and *haima* indicate our pre-translation bodies or the bodies we currently posses that are corruptible. We do not obtain incorruptible bodies until we are changed at the second coming of Christ.

The Gospels give a particularly kingdom obsessed view of the apostles. At different times they ask for signs or who will sit at Christ's right hand. In one instance, Christ very clearly answered their questions, but they perceived it not. He said in John 14:1-3, "Let not your heart be troubled: ye believe in God, believe also in me. In my Father's house are many mansions: if it were not so I would have told you. I go to prepare a place for you. And if I go and prepare a place for you, I will come again, and receive you unto myself; that where I am there ye may be also. And wither I go ye know, and they way ye know." He says, not that He will come to a kingdom they have prepared or established, but rather that He will come and receive them to Him to a place He prepared that where He is there they may be also.

Right before He is about to be carried up into heaven, they ask Jesus whether He is now going to restore the kingdom to Israel, he says, "It is not for you to know the times or the seasons, which the Father hath put in his own power. But ye shall receive power, after that the Holy Ghost is come upon you: ye shall be witnesses unto me both in Jerusalem, and in all Judaea and to Samaria and unto the uttermost part of the earth." In other words, Jesus was telling them that it was not for them to know where and when God would do what He had to do, but they were going to receive power, through the Holy Ghost, that they were supposed to use to take the gospel of Jesus to the entire world. However, the angel who addresses them as they stand staring up into heaven gives them a hint, “This same Jesus, which is taken up from you into heaven, shall so come in like manner as ye have seen him go into heaven.” Here the angel echoes the answer Jesus gave them before: “I will come again.”

More scriptural evidence that a literal kingdom is not to be established before Christ returns is Ezekiel 21: 25-27. "And thou profane wicked prince of Israel, whose day is come, when iniquity shall have an end, Thus saith the Lord God; remove the diadem, and take off the crown: this shall not be the same: exalt them that is low, and abase him that is high. I will overturn, overturn, overturn it; and it shall be no more, until he comes whose right it is; and I will give it him." When we inherit the kingdom it will be when Christ is crowned king and the diadem is claimed by "He whose right it is."

In *Prophets and Kings, pg. 451*, Ellen G. White agrees, “To the ‘profane wicked prince’ had come the day of final reckoning. ‘Remove the diadem,’ the Lord decreed, ‘and take off the crown.’ Not until Christ Himself should set up His kingdom was Judah again to be permitted to have a king. ‘I will overturn, overturn, overturn, it,’ was the divine edict concerning the throne of the house of David; ‘and it shall be no more, until He come whose right it is; and I will give it Him.’ Ezekiel 21:25-27.” She also says, “The Disciples of Christ were looking for the immediate coming of the kingdom of His glory, but in giving them this prayer [the Lord’s Prayer] Jesus taught that the kingdom was not then to be established. They were to pray for its coming as an event yet future. But this petition was also an assurance to them. While they were not to behold the coming of the kingdom in their day, the fact that Jesus made them pray for it is evidence that in God's own time it will surely come…The kingdom of God's grace is now being established, as day by day hearts that have been full of sin and rebellion yield to the sovereignty of His love. But the full establishment of the kingdom of His glory will not take place until the second coming of Christ to this world.”--*Thoughts from the Mount of Blessing, pg. 108.*

The theory of a pre-millennial kingdom not only places a king over Israel before the diadem is returned, but it also denies what scriptures say clearly. In that it also disagrees with Ellen G. White is yet another way that Houteff's claims that his writings are in full agreement with scripture and White's writings are proved to be false.

The first few points dealing with Daniel will be dealt with in the Daniel study presented later, but under point 3 number 3 the statement is made, "The stone was a kingdom before it smote the image (verse 44) and it (the kingdom) shall destroy all these kingdoms...This proves that the kingdom is established before the finishing of the gospel."

There are several problematic portions to this conclusion. First, the fact that the stone was a kingdom before it smote the image and that it shall destroy all these kingdoms doesn't prove that the literal kingdom is established before the finishing of the gospel. The spiritual kingdom is being established through the gospel, so even it is not fully established until the close of probation. The literal kingdom does not have to be established before the finishing of the gospel in order to destroy all the other kingdoms.

Both Scripture and Ellen G. White tell us that after the close of probation there will be a time where the inhabitants of God will stand without a mediator between God and man. We do not know when that time will be and the wicked will not perceive it. Once the close of probation takes place the gospel, has been presented to all and they have had the opportunity to make their yes, yes and their no, no. The kings of the earth will still be actively trying to overthrow God's people, but Christ will return and take His children away from this earth. The vision here mentioned says something very important that cannot be over looked. Daniel 2:35 says, "Then was the iron, the clay, the brass, the silver, and the gold, broken to pieces **together** and became like the chaff of the summer threshingfloors; and the wind carried them away, that **no place was found for them**, and the stone that smote the image became a great mountain, and filled the whole earth."

The kingdoms which the statue represented were broken to pieces *together* and *no place was found for them.* According to Adventist doctrine, the only time when all of those kingdoms represented will be present together will be at the second resurrection and final judgment prior to the establishment of the New Earth where New Jerusalem will be. As the earth will be filled with God's kingdom there will be no place left for them. This information then lends more so to fulfillment after Christ's coming than before. The "ten toe" kings will be alive at the final pronouncement of their judgment so it will be in the days of those kings, and the kingdom of God will not exist on the same earth with them for any length of time because it says that no place was found for them.

Nothing under point 5 is impossible without a pre-millennial kingdom. The verse used, Hosea 3:4, 5 can easily apply to the Dark Ages when the gospel was withheld from the people and they wandered with no true direction. Says White, "Today, the church of God is free to carry forward to completion the divine plan for the salvation of a lost race. For many centuries God's people suffered a restriction of their liberties. The preaching of the gospel in its purity was prohibited, and the severest of penalties were visited upon those who dared disobey the mandates of men. As a consequence, the Lord's great moral vineyard was almost wholly unoccupied. The people were deprived of the light of God's word. The darkness of error and superstition threatened to blot out a knowledge of true religion. God's church on earth was as verily in captivity during this long period of relentless persecution as were the children of Israel held captive in Babylon during the period of the exile."--*Prophets and Kings, pg. 714.*

In point 6 the following conclusion is made based on Isaiah 11:1-12, "This passage could not be referring to Heaven during the millennium or to the New Earth because: a. There will be no Gentiles to seek the kingdom, b. No such gathering described in verses 11, 12 will take place in Heaven or the New Earth. c. There will be no births in the New Earth. Hence, there will be no children. **1SM 172, 173; Luke 20:27-36**

2. Therefore Isaiah here must be speaking of a time when there will be Gentiles seeking to join God's kingdom, and a great gathering from various nations, and when sucking, weaned, and little children exist."

The problem here is that verses 1-5, and 10 are unmistakably talking about Jesus. Harmony must exist in the flow of the chapter, and while Houteff would like to presume that this harmony is established by accepting the pre-millennial kingdom theory, this is not the case. As we have previously established, Jesus is now acting as our High Priest and is ministering in the Most Holy Place. Since we know that the same things patterned in the earthly sanctuary happen in the heavenly, we know that Christ will not leave the Most Holy Place until the sins of all have been either covered by His blood or left exposed because they did not accept His sacrifice. Because of this we know that Gentiles will not be seeking to join God's kingdom after he has exited the sanctuary because the door will already be closed and they will have squandered their probationary time.

While it is partly true that no gathering such as described in verse 11, 12 takes place in Heaven or New Earth, a pre-millennial kingdom is not the answer to the problem. As the gospel is being preached to the entire world, God is gathering together His people from all over the earth as they accept the truth of the gospel into their hearts. I used the words "partly true" because what is heaven, but a gathering of God's remnant from the four corners of the earth into one place? Even as a great multitude they are still the remnant of all those God made and offered salvation to. They are the only ones who accepted the gift and stayed faithful until the end.

Concerning the children and sucklings; Isaiah's vision was written in his own words in a way that was intended to inspire the Israelites to hope and renew their allegiance to God. The possibility that he chose wording reflecting this is strong. While Ellen G. White says there will not be births in on the new earth, she also mentions children on the new earth in many of her visions. She speaks of a company they encounter with red rims on their garments that are explained to be martyrs. She then says that there was a great company of little ones with them. We do not know how our incorruptible pre-fallen condition will affect how we age and look, so Isaiah could only describe what he saw in terms he understood.

False belief or doctrine is often founded on a misapplication of scripture or a misunderstanding of scripture. One of the misapplications of scripture the pre-millennial kingdom belief is based on hinges on Houteff's personal interpretation of Nebuchadnezzar's dream recorded in Daniel 2.

The main problem here is that Nebuchadnezzar's dream had already been interpreted through Daniel: that interpretation coming straight from God. There are several instances where Houteff takes interpreted dreams or visions and reinterprets them to fit his theories (i.e., Ezekiel's vision in Ezekiel 37,Pharoh's dreams in Genesis 41). There is no precedent in scriptures for reinterpreting dreams that have already been given their interpretation and while new truths can always be gleaned from the treasures within the bible, they remain in harmony with the old truths and do not contradict them.

Scripture already provides evidence that a pre-millennial kingdom is not biblical. However, with many false doctrines it can appear that there is biblical evidence to support them as well. Another study on the same Shepherd's Rod website follows this logic:

THE MIGHTY STONE AND THE GREAT IMAGE DANIEL 2
(Outline # 1)
MEDITATION : CW 35 ; CSW 28, 29 (or choose another).

INTRODUCTION:
The study concerning The Great Image of Daniel 2 is a common and generally understood portion of Scripture. It reveals to us through symbols and figures the world's history from the days of king Nebuchadnezzar 'till the close of time. Nevertheless, our focus will be centered on that portion of the king's vision, which is not normally discussed.

REVIEW : Verses 1-27 (verbally). Refresh the memory.

1. Read : Verse 28
Emphasize that the vision reaches its complete fulfillment in our time, and that the message is mainly for those living in the last days, i.e. **Dan. 12:4; PK 547, 548** --- for the latter days.

2. Read : Verses 31-35. The actual vision.
a Explain briefly the meaning of the various parts of the Image.
b Point out that we are living in the days of the ten toes. **1T 361.**
c Especially point out the work of the stone.

3. Where Did The Stone Come From ? ----- The Mountain
Read : Daniel 2:45.
a The stone came from a mountain.
b If the image (gold, silver, brass, stone, etc.) is symbolical then the mountain must also be symbolical.

4. What Does A Mountain Symbolize In Scripture ? ----- People
Read : Dan. 9:16,20.
a Daniel in his prayer likens the church (Jerusalem) to a mountain.
b It could not be a literal mountain, because a literal mountain cannot sin.
Read: Isaiah 2:2,3.
a God here shows that in the last days He will exalt His church above all other churches and kingdoms.
b Also, many people will be invited by the saints to join the true church. **Rev. 18:4** -- The finishing of the Gospel.
Further proof: Isa. 56:7, 2:2; Mic. 4:1-4; Rev. 17:9; Zech. 8:3; Matt. 5:14; Jer. 51:25; Isa. 51:16

5. Exactly What Church Does The Mountain Symbolize? ---SDA
a It must be the church in the latter days (**v. 28**). **I T 361**.
b The church of Laodicea (**Rev. 3:14 -17**).

6. Could Not The Mountain Include The Churches Of The World? ---NO

a God has had only one church in each era. That is the Israelites.
b According to **Rev. 14:8,** Babylon (The churches of the world) has fallen, indicating that God's Spirit has been withdrawn from them. God does however have faithful people in these churches, but they will be brought into the S.D.A. church. See **EW 33; John10:16.**

7. What Or Whom Does The Stone Symbolize?
a A remnant of the remnant church
b If the mountain is people, then the stone must symbolize people as well, for the stone was cut out from the mountain.

8. Cannot The Stone Symbolize Christ At His Second Coming?
a The Stone came from the church (mountain), not heaven or the sky. **Dan. 2:45**
b If the mountain is people the stone must be people too.
c The stone grows and becomes a Great Mountain -- great church. This is done through His people. **Dan. 2: 45**
d The growth of the stone reveals the rapid growth of the purified church (the stone). It indicates that many, many, new converts will join the ranks of the true people of God. This cannot happen at the second visible return of Christ, for the gospel would have already been completed, probation closed, and the plagues fallen.

For purposes of this book the main focus will be on those portions of this study that seek to support the pre-millennial kingdom belief.

To start out Daniel 12:4 "But thou, O Daniel, shut up the words, and seal the book, even to the time of the end:" does not apply to Nebuchadnezzar's dream. We know this because while the visions given Daniel were not fully explained, Nebuchadnezzar's dream was. Also, the order God gave Daniel to seal up the book would not apply to Nebuchadnezzar's dream as by then Nebuchadnezzar's kingdom was already past and he dead. Also Daniel 2:45 says, "Forasmuch as thou sawest that the stone was cut out of the mountain without hands, and that it brake in pieces the iron, the brass, the clay, the silver, and the gold; the great God hath made known to the king what shall come to pass hereafter: and the dream is certain, and the interpretation thereof sure." The dream therefore was for Nebuchadnezzar's benefit and while we glean confirmation of this dream in our earth's history, it does not join Daniel's particular visions in importance to the end times.

The reference to EGW writings, *Prophets and Kings, pg. 547, 548*, upon inspection will reveal agreement with this understanding. "'The wise shall understand', was spoken of the visions of Daniel that were to be unsealed in the latter days." She specifically refers to the visions of Daniel, not the vision of Nebuchadnezzar.

Nebuchadnezzar's vision had already received its interpretation by God through Daniel. Knowing this shows that the rest of the study is based solely on what Houteff has taught concerning the scripture and not the interpretation already given by God. Points 3-6 on the study are theories based on Houteff's understanding of the 144,000, but then on point 7 the study redirects to scripture with the question, "What Or Whom Does The Stone Symbolize?" Point 7, however, does not use scripture to support the statements found underneath. It draws its conclusions from the process explained in points 3-6.

The scriptures on the other hand say the stone represents God's kingdom. Daniel 2:24, 35 says "Thou sawest till that a stone was cut out without hands, which smote the image upon his feet that were of iron and clay, and brake them to pieces. Then was the iron, the clay, the brass, the silver, and the gold, broken to pieces together, and became like the chaff of the summer threshingfloors; and the wind carried them away, that no place was found for them: and the stone that smote the image became a great mountain, and filled the whole earth." In interpreting the dream he says in verse 44, " And in the days of these kings shall the God of heaven set up a kingdom, which shall never be destroyed: and the kingdom shall not be left to other people, but it shall break in pieces and consume all these kingdoms, and it shall stand for ever."

Point 8 is difficult to follow in that it asks the question, "Cannot The Stone Symbolize Christ At His Second Coming?" There is no precedent in scripture or traditional Adventist thought that the stone symbolizes Christ. The difference in opinion here is not what the stone represents. Scripture identifies it as a kingdom as does Ellen G. White and Houteff. The difference is when the kingdom is believed to be established and scripture has shown that to be at and not before the second coming of Christ. One thing is certain! Regardless of when the Jews expected the establishment of the promised kingdom, they did not expect it to be established without Christ. Neither did the Apostles and neither, as Adventists, do we.

The tongue of the wise useth knowledge aright: but the mouth of fools poureth out foolishness. Proverbs 15:2

Chapter 5

I mentioned before when addressing the Daniel 2 study that Houteff makes a habit of re-interpreting some of the dreams given in scripture to meet his purpose. One such dream is the dream given to Pharaoh that Joseph was called upon to interpret. One important thing about each of these dreams is that in Daniel's and Joseph's case they each told their respective kings that God had given the dreams to each king for that particular king. Daniel says, "the great God hath made known to the king what shall come to pass hereafter: and the dream is certain and the interpretation is sure." Joseph says, "It is not in me: God shall give Pharaoh an answer of peace....And Joseph said unto Pharaoh, The dream of Pharaoh is one: God hath shewed Pharaoh what He is about to do."

In both instances God is given the credit for producing the interpretation and both Daniel and Joseph make a point of telling the kings that their dreams were from God informing them of what was to come.

In the opening portions of the Shepherd's Rod message Houteff makes this statement about Pharaoh's vision,

> "The symbol can represent only one thing, and that is the world's history in two great divisions of time; namely B.C. and A.D. with the cross (Christ) as the dividing line. 'For all the prophets and the law prophesied until John.' It is for this reason Jesus made the statement for we have no other thus far. The years of plenty is B.C. in which time God gave plenty to supply the world's need for the years of famine (New Testament time A.D.). As Joseph gathered the corn into the storehouses by his servants, -- the Egyptians, just so Christ gather the Word of God (spiritual food) in the Bible (the storehouse) by His servants, the prophets. 'God who at sundry times and in divers manners

spake in time past unto the fathers by the prophets, hath in these last days spoken unto us by His Son, whom He hath appointed heir of all things, by whom also He made the worlds.' Heb. 1:1, 2. Had it not been for this purpose then we ask, what could it have been for? God who was responsible for the event did it not to bring hardships to His subjects, or to starve the world, as the famine was not in Egypt only, for we read, 'And the famine was over all the face of the earth.' Gen. 41:56. Had this not been the symbol, why would God have brought the famine over all the earth? Some people may have difficulty in being convinced, and others can never be convinced, but the harmony of the lesson can hardly be questioned. If the seven years of plenty and the seven years of famine are not a type of the world's history; Joseph's immense storehouses not a type of the Bible; the corn gathered in the seven years of plenty not a type of Word in the Bible; the feeding of the world not a type of the New Testament time consuming the Scriptures gathered in the Old Testament time; then we ask, Where are the types of all these events? Has not God given the gospel in types as well as in prophecy? 'Christ was the foundation of the Jewish economy. The whole system of types and symbols was compacted prophecy of the gospel, a presentation in which were bound up the promises of redemption.' Acts of the Apostles, page 14. If the seven years of plenty and the seven years of famine did not represent the world's history, the coincident as well shall endeavor to bring forth could hardly have been possible by an accident."-*The Shepherd's Rod, Vol. 1, p.19.*

There is nothing in the entire book of Genesis or the remainder of the Bible, for that matter, that even suggests that this could be true. Houteff creates a theory and bases the rest of his conclusions on it, plugging on as if the theory were fact instead of something he made up.

The idea that B.C. and A.D. are respectively the seven years of plenty and the seven years of famine is in no way reflected in scripture. While Houteff claims the need of type/anti-type to make the picture perfect, the dream gives the type and God through Joseph gives the anti-type. The type is the seven fat and seven lean cows and the seven full heads of corn and the seven sparse ones. They anti-type is the seven years of plenty and seven years of famine. The type and anti-type is already given. Nowhere in scripture does the anti-type become type again in order to make way for another anti-type as Houteff is trying to establish here.

Lets break down this excerpt and see what happens to the theory. Houteff says first, "The symbol can represent only one thing, and that is the world's history in two great divisions of time; namely B.C. and A.D. with the cross (Christ) as the dividing line. 'For all the prophets and the law prophesied until John.' It is for this reason Jesus made the statement for we have no other thus far." He says that his theory is the reason why Jesus made the statement he did because "we have no other thus far." Houteff is quoting Matthew 11:13 here. While Houteff says we have no reason for this statement save his theory, if one reads the chapter in its entirety, it can be found that this is not true. Jesus made this statement to verify that John was who he claimed to be, the one preparing the way of the Lord. Jesus is saying here that the law and the prophets have prophesied up to John the Baptist and that He is the fulfillment of that prophecy. Not that after John there would be a famine in terms of the availability to the Word of God.

In fact it would make more sense to flip Houteff's theory. It is during Houteff's proclaimed years of famine that the Messiah appeared and opened up the reality that salvation was also available to the Gentiles and thus the whole world. It was Jesus' life that opened up the scriptures to the common man so that all could see the words of scripture come alive. While Houteff calls the years in and after Christ came to earth as God manifest in the flesh famine years, the Samaritan woman at the well was introduced to the Living Water that would cause her never to thirst again, and many others were offered the Bread of Life.

In other words while before the plan of salvation was understood strictly amongst the Jews as revealed in the sanctuary service, Christ's appearance opened the floodgates revealing that He came to save all those who were lost and thus providing a bountiful harvest where before the fields gave up few.

The next portion of Houteff's theory is, "As Joseph gathered the corn into the storehouses by his servants, -- the Egyptians, just so Christ gather the Word of God (spiritual food) in the Bible (the storehouse) by His servants, the prophets." Here it is important to understand the type/anti-type formula. A type and anti-type example had a relationship involved. Let me give you an example. In the sanctuary service the lamb (and various other sacrifices) was the type of Christ in that the lamb represented Christ and the purpose He would fulfill when coming to earth. One thing that is most important to note though is that in order for the lamb to be a true type it had to represent Christ in every way. In other words, the lamb had to be perfect with no defects. It could not be crippled or in any other way inferior. It was to be spotless and pure. Only after it passed a rigorous inspection could the lamb be used as an acceptable sacrifice to represent Christ.

Knowing this makes Houteff's theory, that Joseph gathering corn by his servants (the Egyptians) represents Christ gathering the Word of God in the Bible by His servants (the prophets), fall apart. The Egyptian servants doing Joseph's bidding cannot represent the prophets of God because the Egyptians were a heathen nation who worshipped the sun and many other gods. They did not recognize Joseph's God as their own and even viewed Pharaoh as a god. God's servants on the other hand were dedicated to His service and had no god, but the God of Heaven. Therefore a perfect relationship between type and anti-type does not exist here.

Another point is that Jesus was not gathering Himself (He is the Word of God) into the Bible through His prophets. He was informing His people of what to look for in order to recognize Him when He came. They did not "store up" what God revealed to them about His first coming and that is why no one was prepared for His arrival. In order for Houteff's theory to hold true, the Jews, at least, should have all been ready for His arrival and been the first to benefit from His appearance encouraged by their leaders to go to Christ (the Egyptians were informed of the reason for the storing of the grain and came willingly throughout the famine to receive food when their leaders let them know it was available) and know exactly where to go to access Him and spread the word of where He was (when the famine began the people knew exactly where to go for food). Instead the Jews were trying to keep the news of Jesus quiet. They were trying to sabotage His ministry and they definitely weren't informing the people that they would find the Bread of Life in Christ.

Houteff goes on to say, "Had it not been for this purpose then we ask, what could it have been for? God who was responsible for the event did it not to bring hardships to His subjects, or to starve the world, as the famine was not in Egypt only, for we read, 'And the famine was over all the face of the earth.' Gen. 41:56. Had this not been the symbol, why would God have brought the famine over all the earth? Some people may have difficulty in being convinced, and others can never be convinced, but the harmony of the lesson can hardly be questioned. If the seven years of plenty and the seven years of famine are not a type of the world's history; Joseph's immense storehouses not a type of the Bible; the corn gathered in the seven years of plenty not a type of Word in the Bible; the feeding of the world not a type of the New Testament time consuming the Scriptures gathered in the Old Testament time; then we ask, Where are the types of all these events?"

Houteff presents the question, what could it have been for, this dream given to Pharaoh, if not for the theory he presents? The answer is given not only in scripture, but also by Ellen G. White. Joseph had been given dreams much earlier in life concerning his brothers and father bowing before him. While he'd been criticized for it and failed himself to see the meaning of it until seeing his brothers again when they came for corn during the famine, God had already revealed to Abraham that his seed would experience slavery and then be delivered. God's purpose in this was manifold. As these prophecies became manifest He wanted the children of Israel to remember how He had provided for them through Joseph and use that example as encouragement and hope to get through the hard times ahead. He also wanted to show Himself to the Egyptians as the God over all as Ellen G. White gives hint to in this quote,

> "It was God's design that through Joseph, Bible religion should be introduced among the Egyptians. This faithful witness was to represent Christ in the court of kings. Through dreams, God communicated with Joseph in his youth, giving him an intimation of the high position he would be called to fill. The brothers of Joseph, to prevent the fulfillment of his dreams, sold him as a slave, but their cruel act resulted in bringing about the very thing the dreams had foretold.
>
> "Those who seek to turn aside the purpose of God, and oppose His will, may appear for a time to prosper; but God is at work to fulfill His own purposes, and He will make manifest who is the ruler of the heavens and the earth.
>
> "Joseph regarded his being sold into Egypt as the greatest calamity that could have befallen him; but he saw the necessity of trusting in God as he had never done when protected by his father's love. Joseph brought God with him into Egypt, and the fact was made apparent by his cheerful demeanor amid his sorrow. As the ark of God brought rest and prosperity to Israel, so did this God-loving, God-fearing youth bring a blessing to Egypt. This was manifested in so marked a manner that Potiphar, in whose house he served, attributed all his blessings to his purchased slave, and made him a son rather than a servant. It is God's purpose that those who love and honor His name shall be honored also themselves, and that the glory given to God through them shall be reflected upon themselves.

"Joseph's character did not change when he was exalted to a position of trust. He was brought where his virtue would shine in distinct light in good works. The blessing of God rested upon him in the house and in the field. All the responsibilities of Potiphar's house were placed upon him. And in all this he manifested steadfast integrity; for he loved and feared God."--*Youth's Instructor*, Mar. 11, 1897.

Joseph's life, according to Ellen G. White illustrated Christ's. She says in *Patriarchs and Prophets, pg. 239, 240*:

"The life of Joseph illustrates the life of Christ. It was envy that moved the brothers of Joseph to sell him as a slave; they hoped to prevent him from becoming greater than themselves. And when he was carried to Egypt, they flattered themselves that they were to be no more troubled with his dreams, that they had removed all possibility of their fulfillment. But their own course was overruled by God to bring about the very event that they designed to hinder. So the Jewish priests and elders were jealous of Christ, fearing that He would attract the attention of the people from them. They put Him to death, to prevent Him from becoming king, but they were thus bringing about this very result.

"Joseph, through his bondage in Egypt, became a savior to his father's family; yet this fact did not lessen the guilt of his brothers. So the crucifixion of Christ by His enemies made Him the Redeemer of mankind, the Saviour of the fallen race, and Ruler over the whole world; but the crime of His murderers was just as heinous as though God's providential hand had not controlled events for His own glory and the good of man.

"As Joseph was sold to the heathen by his own brothers, so Christ was sold to His bitterest enemies by one of His disciples. Joseph was falsely accused and thrust into

> prison because of his virtue; so Christ was despised and rejected because His righteous, self-denying life was a rebuke to sin; and though guilty of no wrong, He was condemned upon the testimony of false witnesses. And Joseph's patience and meekness under injustice and oppression, his ready forgiveness and noble benevolence toward his unnatural brothers, represent the Saviour's uncomplaining endurance of the malice and abuse of wicked men, and His forgiveness, not only of His murderers, but of all who have come to Him confessing their sins and seeking pardon."

To his last question, "What are the types to all these events?" the answer refers back to what was said earlier. The aspects of the dream were the types and the fulfillment in the actual years of surplus and famine were the anti-type.

Without trying to mix Houteff's theory into an already clear subject, the quote he uses by Ellen G. White to substantiate his theory can easily be understood put back in its proper context. He quotes her words in Acts of the Apostles, but not all of them, "*Through the teachings of the sacrificial service, Christ was to be uplifted before all nations, and all who would look to Him should live.* Christ was the foundation of the Jewish economy. The whole system of types and symbols was compacted prophecy of the gospel, a presentation in which were bound up the promises of redemption."--*Acts of the Apostles, pg. 14.*Even when looking at the just portion of the quote he used one notices that she says the *Jewish economy.* This was addressed when we dealt with Houteff's secondfruits theory. After reading the sentence that immediately precedes the quote, it is placed back into its rightful context. She is talking of the Jewish economy not about the Egyptian economy to which no types have ever applied. It is in the Jewish economy, the sacrificial service, that we see the types to which Christ is the anti-type. This applies in no way to the types in the dream of Pharaoh.

Earlier in the same passage Ellen G. White says,

"From the beginning God has wrought through His people to bring blessing to the world. To the ancient Egyptian nation God made Joseph a fountain of life. Through the integrity of Joseph the life of that whole people was preserved. Through Daniel God saved the life of all the wise men of Babylon. And these deliverances are as object lessons; they illustrate the spiritual blessings offered to the world through connection with the God whom Joseph and Daniel worshiped. Everyone in whose heart Christ abides, everyone who will show forth His love to the world, is a worker together with God for the blessing of humanity. As he receives from the Saviour grace to impart to others, from his whole being flows forth the tide of spiritual life. God chose Israel to reveal His character to men. He desired them to be as wells of salvation in the world. To them were committed the oracles of heaven, the revelation of God's will. In the early days of Israel the nations of the world, through corrupt practices, had lost the knowledge of God. They had once known Him; but because "they glorified Him not as God, neither were thankful; but became vain in their imaginations . . . their foolish heart was darkened." Romans 1:21. Yet in His mercy God did not blot them out of existence. He purposed to give them an opportunity of again becoming acquainted with Him through His chosen people. Through the teachings of the sacrificial service, Christ was to be uplifted before all nations, and all who would look to Him should live. Christ was the foundation of the Jewish economy. The whole system of types and symbols was a compacted prophecy of the gospel, a presentation in which were bound up the promises of redemption."

Yet another dream that he puts his personal take on is the vision God interprets in Ezekiel 37. Houteff believes that the vision related is a literal one and that the house of Israel described here will be led by David into the pre-millennial kingdom. There is a confusing portion here in that they also believe that an anti-typical David will rule the pre-millennial kingdom, not the literal one and not Jesus. This causes the David mentioned here to be a symbolic one, rendering exactly one verse out of the whole chapter symbolic while the rest are believed to be literal.

The problems with this interpretation are just as numerous as the other problems with Houteff's conclusions. First and most importantly what must be acknowledged is that the interpretation here is not given by God through man, but by God directly to man.

Let's break down the chapter. First, Ezekiel says, "The hand of the Lord was upon me, and carried me out in the spirit of the Lord and set me down in the midst of the valley which was full of bones, and caused me to pass by them round about: and, behold, there were very many in the open valley; and, lo, they were very dry. And he said unto me, Son of man, can these bones live? And I answered, O lord God, though knowest." In the first three verses Ezekiel is telling us what is happening and relating a conversation between he and God that was initiated by God. God asks him if the bones can live, and Ezekiel responds only God knows. We must recognize that Ezekiel is relating what he saw and then relating the subsequent conversation between he and God.

God then says, "Prophesy upon these bones, and say unto them, O ye dry bones, hear the world of the Lord. Thus saith the Lord God unto these bones; behold, I will cause breath to enter into you, and ye shall live: And I will lay sinews upon you, and will bring up flesh upon you, and cover you with skin, and put breath in you, and ye shall live; and ye shall know that I am the Lord." Ezekiel relates that he did what the Lord said and as he was prophesying the exact thing that God said would happen happened at that moment except the breath entering them. Then God says, "Prophesy unto the wind, prophesy, son of man, and say to the wind, Thus saith the Lord God; Come from the four winds, O breath, and breath upon these slain, that they may live." Again Ezekiel relates that he did what the Lord said to do and that "breath came into them, and they lived and stood up upon their feet, and exceeding great army."

In verse 11 God begins to explain to Ezekiel what everything that he has observed and taken part in means, in other words, he interprets what the symbols mean. God says, "Son of man, these bones are the whole house of Israel: behold they say, Our bones are dried, and our hope is lost: we are cut off for our parts. Therefore prophesy and say unto them, Thus saith the Lord God; Behold, O my people, I will open your graves and cause you to come up out of your graves, and bring you into the land of Israel. And ye shall know that I am the Lord, when I have opened your graves, O my people and brought you up out of your graves, and shall put my spirit in you, and ye shall live, and I shall place you in your own land: then shall ye know that I the Lord have spoken it, and performed it, saith the Lord."

Here the pattern is broken. Ezekiel says nothing to the whole house of Israel who is living and breathing in front of him an "exceeding great army." This is a clear indication that this chapter is describing something symbolic rather than literal. Without following God's instructions, seemingly, Ezekiel receives another word from the Lord. God says, "Moreover, thou son of man, take thee one stick, and write upon it, For Judah, and for the children of Israel his companions: and take another stick and write upon it, For Joseph, the stick of Ephraim and for all the house of Israel his companions: And join them one to another into one stick; and they shall become one in thine hand. And when the children of thy people shall speak unto thee, saying, Wilt thou not shew us what thou meanest by these? Say unto them, Thus saith the Lord God; Behold, I will take the stick of Joseph which is in the hand of Ephraim and the tribes of Israel his fellows, and will put them with him, even with the stick of Judah, and make them one stick, and they shall be one in mine hand. And the sticks whereon thou writest shall be in thine hand before their eyes." The rest of the chapter is God speaking to Ezekiel and the great army that was raised up is no longer mentioned. Later in verses 24 through 28, God says, "And David my servant shall be king over them; and they all shall have one shepherd: they shall also walk in my judgments, and observe my statues, and do them. And they shall dwell in the land that I have given unto Jacob my servant, where in your fathers have dwelt; and they shall dwell therein, even they, and their children, and their children's children for ever; and my servant David shall be their prince forever. Moreover I will make a covenant of peace with them; it shall be an everlasting covenant with them: and will place them, and multiply them, and will set my sanctuary in the midst of them for evermore. My tabernacle also shall be with them: yea, I will be their God, and they shall be my people. And the heathen shall know that I the Lord do sanctify Israel, when my sanctuary shall be in the midst of them for evermore."

While Houteff wants to attribute this to a literal resurrection, the message is clear, if read in context, that God is speaking to Ezekiel about a spiritually dead Israel, not a literally dead Israel. The dead dry bones are described as talking to Ezekiel not the living ones. Through the vision God gives an imagery of what He plans to do with Israel. He plans to raise them from their spiritual death and give them the promises He describes.

That Ezekiel leaves off talking to the exceeding great army also lends to the fact that this was imagery rather than a literal resurrection.

Then turn attention to the last few verses. Here David is described as a King, a prince, and a shepherd. While David was a shepherd and a King, he was never a prince. However, Jesus, the Son of David, holds title to all three. He is the Good Shepherd, He is the Prince of Peace, and He is the King of Kings.

One must understand that the promises of God are conditional for us based on how we respond to God. God never breaks His covenant with us, but we often and frequently break our covenant with Him. Israel never successfully held up their covenant with God and so He was never able to follow through with this promise for them, but as the Scriptures tell us, we are to inherit the promises God gave, and Ellen G. White shares with us, the promises unfulfilled with Ancient Israel will be fulfilled with

Spiritual Israel. “If we comply with the conditions God laid down for Israel, if we come before God in the beauty of holiness, and worship Him in Spirit and in truth, we shall receive the blessings that God promised to them. God sends His Word to assure us that if we will be obedient to Him, He will acknowledge us as members of His royal family. He will honor His peculiar people above all nations. ‘This honour have all His saints’ (Psalm 149:9).”--*Manuscript Releases, Vol. 1, No. 31 - The Covenants, pg. 108.*

Men and brethren, let me freely speak unto you of the patriarch David, that he is both dead and buried, and his sepulchre is with us unto this day....Therefore let all the house of Israel know assuredly, that God hath made that same Jesus, whom ye have crucified, both Lord and Christ. Acts 2:29,33

Chapter 6

One cannot miss the parallels between the Anti-typical David teaching of Victor Houteff and that of the Catholic position concerning the pope. The gist of Houteff's teaching is that prior to Christ's visual second coming He will come invisibly and reign in combination with a visible king, chosen by the 144,000, in the pre-millennial kingdom. The invisible Christ and visible anti-typical David would form what, Houteff describes as an ensign. Not only does this go completely against the words of the angel who told the disciples Christ would return in the same manner He left, but it more damagingly goes against Christ's words that His return would be visible to all, as lightening is seen in the sky from the east to the west.

Just as compelling is this question, if the choosing of a king by ancient Israel was rejecting God's authority and right to rule His people, would not the same be the case for modern Israel? Ancient Israel wished to emulate the kingdoms around them. How does the exact same act by Modern Israel in order to establish the pre-millennial kingdom turn into something positive? What is the need for a visible king to rule in conjunction with Christ invisible when God has lead us without a visible king up to now, and, had Ancient Israel not rejected His authority, would have done the same with them?

Also, as mentioned earlier, Ezekiel 21:24-27 says that the diadem removed when Israel was ultimately taken out of power will not be returned until He whose right it is to take it comes and God gives it to Him. Because God is the giver of the kingdom, it is logical that God is the possessor. Scripture says He will give Christ the throne of His father David. Doesn't that then point to

Jesus as the anti-typical David and not some human chosen to represent Him? Acts 2:29, 30 says:"Men and brethren, let me speak freely unto you of the patriarch David, that he is both dead and buried, and his sepulcher is with us unto this day. Therefore being a prophet, and knowing that God had sworn with an oath to him, that of the fruit of his loins, according to the flesh, He would raise up Christ to sit on his throne."

Believing there will be a human, visible representative of Christ on earth while He reigns invisibly sounds almost identical to the catholic view of the pope as the Vicar of Christ. According to dictionary.com *vicar* means: "A person who acts in place of another; substitute and a person who is authorized to perform the functions of another; deputy: *God's vicar on earth.*" This visible king would be someone to represent Christ in bodily form. However, Christ already has a body. He did not divest of it upon returning to heaven. He is in bodily form interceding for us in the sanctuary as our High Priest, and will reign, in bodily form, not invisibly.

The Anti-typical David teaching is also known as the ensign teaching and finds its origin in how Houteff understands chapter 11 of Isaiah. Part of the reasoning Houteff uses to support this teaching is reflected in his quote that, "Since therefore from the 'stem' of Jesse came the 'rod' (David), and from the rod sprang the Branch (Christ), David the visible king and Christ the invisible King of kings shall 'in that day' -- in our time -- constitute the 'ensign,' and 'to it shall the Gentiles seek: and His rest [or His resting place, -- the location where the 'rod' or ensign stands -- the kingdom] shall be glorious.' Yea 'I will make the place of My feet glorious' (Isa. 60:13), saith the Lord."-*Tract, No. 8, pg. 47*. However, Isaiah 11:1 does not say that. It says, "And there shall come forth a rod out of the stem of Jesse, and a Branch shall grow out of his roots." While Houteff says the branch sprang from the rod, Isaiah says the Rod came from the stem and the Branch grew out from the root. This is a small, yet significant difference and its importance is found when looking at Revelation 22:16. Here Christ says, "I am the root and the offspring of David." Even more interesting is that just a few verses before He says that He is the Alpha and Omega. Understood together, Isaiah and Revelation are both saying that Christ is the beginning and end as the root and the offspring. He comes both before David and after. These verses establish His authority as God. Both chapters go on to describe Christ as judging in righteousness. Neither mentions this ensign made up of Christ invisible with a human visible counterpart.

The ensign instead is described in verse 10 as the root of Jesse, "And in that day there shall be a root of Jesse, which shall stand for an ensign of the people; to it shall the Gentiles seek: and his rest shall be glorious." In other words, Jesus will be a banner to the people and to him will the Gentiles seek and His rest will be glorious. This reaffirms the Messianic content of this chapter and not the pre-millennial kingdom as put forth by Houteff.

Only let your conversation be as it becometh the gospel of Christ: that whether I come and see you, or else be absent, I may hear of your affairs, that ye stand fast in one spirit, with one mind ***striving together*** *for the faith of the gospel; Phil 1:27*

Chapter 7

While there are many other scriptural points that can be made to uproot the theories that form the foundation of the Shepherd's Rod message, at the end of it all there were two things that God revealed to me that eliminated any remaining doubt that could have llingered. The first one was Houteff's attitude concerning his writings and the way his use of his own writings undermined the foundation of the movement, and the second one was the fragmented existence of the remaining groups of Shepherd's Rod believers and their attitudes toward each other.

Houteff is recorded as saying, "In 1931, after The Shepherd's Rod, Vol. 1, came off the press, we published a two-page article in which we said that what God has led us into is either all truth or no truth. Since that time we have published another book and over twenty tracts besides the series of the *Timely Greetings*, all containing doctrinal matter. These publications have been scattered far and wide throughout the Denomination, but to this day the Denomination has not once officially attempted to refute any subject in its entirety. They ever try to take away what we have on these scriptures, but never give us something better." - *Timely GreetingsVol. 1, No. 18.*

In 1929 and on until 1934[1] when he met before a committee at his request, members of the Denomination approached Victor Houteff (some were even approached by him) to show him the error of his ways, but so convinced was he that he was right, that under the rash claim that he had been led by God into either all truth or none at all, he now bears the responsibility for leading many of God's precious ones astray.

What can be better than the truth? Has it come to a point where the truth is no longer acceptable and so when "better" theories crowd in we should sacrifice truth for lies? Is the best thing than to allow our fellows in Christ to continue down a path undeterred that is riddled with falsehoods just because they do not recognize the simple beauty of the truth? Should we condone friends or the strangers within our gates accepting a lie in place of the truth just because they refuse to see the error? God forbid!

Ellen G. White says, "We are to pray for divine enlightenment, but at the same time we should be careful how we receive everything termed new light. We must beware lest, undercover of searching for new truth, Satan shall divert our minds from Christ and the special truths for this time. I have been shown that it is the device of the enemy to lead minds to dwell upon some obscure or unimportant point, something that is not fully revealed or is not essential to our salvation. This is made the absorbing theme, the 'present truth', when all their investigations and suppositions only serve to make matters more obscure than before, and to confuse the minds of some who ought to be seeking for oneness through sanctification of the truth."--*Selected Messages, Book 1, pg. 159.*

Neither the Scriptures, nor Ellen G. White give us a detailed understanding of the 144,000 yet Houteff focuses largely on the 144,000 and, with no scriptural support for this, makes the understanding of the subject tantamount to an issue that if not understood as he presents it, that will ultimately result in more than half the church being slaughtered, and as a result of rejecting what he holds up as "new light", losing our salvation. One pervading problem that I had is a quote he attributes to Ellen G. White in the beginning portions of his approach to the 144,000 that cannot be found anywhere in her published writings. He says on pg. 13-14 of the Shepherd's Rod, "Sister White had received inspiration on this subject, but, like Daniel, was not permitted to know who, how, and when made, until Gods appointed time. The following is a quotation made by her to Elder E.E. Andross: 'I feel confident, Elder Andross, that the brethren in Southern California will find blessing in reviewing the teachings of Scripture concerning the 144,000 and bringing to bear upon these teachings whatever of light there may be in the published writings of the Spirit of Prophecy, and as prayerful consideration is given the matter in all its bearings, I believe that God will make the truth sufficiently clear to make possible the avoidance of needless and unprofitable questions not vital to the salvation of precious souls.' No matter what combination of words used to search, including 'Elder Andross' a quote like this one is not found. What is found between White and Andross is Andross asking about Adventist doctor's increasing their fees for service. Nevertheless, the subject of the 144,000 is an obscure point that becomes an absorbing theme flowing through almost every theory he presents.

At one time he made the postulation that he believed, given the size of the church at the time, the 144,000 would be approximately one-third of the church.

But most disturbing is the immortal nature Houteff has placed upon the 144,000 a company in which he includes himself. In the Symbolic Code, Volume 3, Numbers 5-6, page 8, Houteff is defending his recent marriage to his followers. A lot of criticism had come his way because of the great age difference between he and his new wife, and the criticism came from those who still believed his claims of being in harmony with Ellen G. White. She advises against a great disparity in age between those who are going to be married. Houteff defends his marriage, saying, "Those who believe in Present Truth, yet continue to find fault with Brother Houteff's marriage, prove to us one of two things: either that they are shallow thinkers, or that they have no faith in what they believe, for the message teaches that we, as a part of the 144,000, shall never die." On other occasions he said,"Keep your knees in motion and let not opportunities be neglected, for the final movements shall be rapid ones. Thus shall you 'walk with God' as Enoch of old, and as he was translated without tasting death so shall you be." He says also, referencing Ellen G. White in the midst, "Moreover, as the Shepherd's Rod is the Elijah message (Testimonies to Ministers, p 475), it is impossible for anyone who accepts it and lives it to die, for the type demands translation. Thus it is that Elijah stands as a type of the 144,000."-*The Symbolic Code, No. 9, March 15, pg.9*. And again, "There is nothing that can take the life of the 144,000."-*The Symbolic Code, Volume 2, Nos. 7-8, pg.11*.

It is prudent to point out the first quote, particularly, in relation to the implications it has for Victor Houteff. He said, "It is impossible for anyone who accepts it and lives it [the Shepherd's Rod message] to die, for the type demands translation." He also said,"If the ministry can prove us wrong on the 144,000, which is the message of the hour, or even on any one topic in our publications, we agree to retract our position and destroy all of our three volumes." There are only two ways to go here. If we are to believe Houteff that it is impossible for anyone who accepts and lives the Shepherd's Rod message to die than there is little choice other than to conclude that Houteff,who died in 1955, did not accept or live the message he himself gave. If we are to believe that Houteff did accept and live his own message, than he was wrong that there was nothing that could take the life of the 144,000 and by his words again, his writings should be destroyed. Did he not consider himself one of the 144,000 his argument postulating that there should be no reason to have issue with his marriage was pointless and just an avoidance of the issue.

The last thing that convinced me was the current state of the Shepherd's Rod movement. While I was involved with Saul he was closely following the Shepherd's Rod focused ministry of Don Adair based in Salem, South Carolina. On his website, www.dividian.org, there are several studies written by him that share some of the beliefs of his section of the Shepherd's Rod movement. They are split up in sections directed to those who are Shepherd's Rod believers, those who are still Adventists, and lastly those who are neither. One of the studies mailed to me directly, entitled, "Who is the Visible King David?", puts forth Adair's theory that Victor Houteff will be resurrected before the end of time and reign as the ensign Anti-typical David in the pre-millennial kingdom.

Saul, who shared with me recently that he doesn't follow Adair's teachings anymore because he believes Adair has added to the Shepherd's Rod unbeknownst to those he shares it with, never gave me a solid opinion on whether he agreed with Adair's theory or not, however,Saul did have a belief of sorts that both Ellen G.White and Victor Houteff would be resurrected prior to the pre-millennial kingdom being established. He shared with me also that Brad[2], the husband of the couple we spent Sabbath afternoons with, did not agree with Don Adair on this issue and was more aligned with the Shepherd's Rod group that was located in the New England area headed by Tony Hibbert in Mountaindale, NY, who names no one in particular as this Anti-typical David.

This got me curious to the fragmented nature of those who claim the Shepherd's Rod message to be their guiding light. There are several names listed as leaders (or former leaders) of various groups of Shepherd's Rod believers: Don Adair, Tony Hibbert, Jemmy Bingham, Norman Archer, Bob and Bonnie Jones, Bobby Conner and Wanda O'Berry (Adair's ex-wife). There was also Florence Houteff (Victor's widow), Ben Roden, and Vernon Howell aka David Koresh.

Each group claims, in its own way, that they are the true Shepherd's Rod group holding in common not much more than the Shepherd's Rod message itself, and disagreeing on numerous different side beliefs. Some believe that Houteff was the last prophet, while others hold that there are many more already prophesying or yet to come. Bob and Bonnie Jones relate prophetic messages on their website that they claim to have received over the years. Don Adair has this statement on his website, "The Davidians are the upshoot from decadent Seventh-day Adventists prophetically envisioned in Ezekiel, chapter nine. Its members are in the main those who have been cast out and deprived of the fellowship of their Seventh-day Adventist churches. Thus being separated from their church and denied its name because of their having given heed to the voice of the Rod, the voice of the Good Shepherd, they are called by the name imbedded in the work of the Rod, 'Davidian Seventh-day

Adventists,' until the time they shall be 'called by a new name, which the mouth of the Lord shall name.' Isa. 62:2."--*The Leviticus Of The Davidian Seventh-day Adventists*, pg. 12:1

The fragmentation of the group started almost immediately after the death of Victor Houteff when his wife took over the leadership of the organization and a power struggle ensued between her and Ben Roden.

One blessing that must be acknowledged here is that Mrs. Houteff eventually remarried and rejoined the Adventist Church.

The Bible says in Matthew 7:15-20, "Beware of false prophets, which come to you in sheep's clothing, but inwardly they are ravening wolves. Ye shall know them by their fruits. Do men gather grapes of thorns, or figs of thistles? Even so every good tree bringeth forth good fruit; but a corrupt tree bringeth forth evil fruit. A good tree cannot bring forth evil fruit, neither can a corrupt tree bring forth good fruit. Every tree that bringeth not forth good fruit is hewn down, and cast into the fire. Wherefore by their fruits ye shall know them."

For me, personally, the current state of the Shepherd's Rod followers and the disconnect that exists from one group to the next is just one more thing that cautions me against finding security in the teachings put forth. Real Truth can both divide and unite! However, in every situation where real truth exists, it divides those who follow it as truth from those who reject it. Truth never fails to unite those who share it. As truth it cannot divide those who share it, yet each Shepherd's Rod group is claiming the name, but not association with each other. They, in fact, subtly undermine the other groups by their claims of being the "only true" or "authentic" groups. The attention then is not placed on the message, but rather on those who carry the message. The lack of unity is a strong indicator of the validity of the message. Houteff's diverse, damaged, and unrelated fruit indicate which kind of tree he was.

Unfortunately, this is not seen amongst those who cling to his theories and the twisted logic that Houteff offers looks to them as a precious thing. When error is pointed out and correction received, it can be overwhelming and shake the very foundation of a person's outlook on their walk with God. They are left questioning how they were so easily led away from God when they thought to be so near to Him. They can experience the same feelings of horror mixed with relief I felt when I realized how far away from God I really was and how thoroughly deceived I had allowed myself to become. There is also the knowledge of the active part one played in overlooking those cautions and warnings God placed in the way to warn of the mistaken direction. Then there are those who choose denial of the error, hoping in vain that there will be some sort of vindication if they hold to the teaching. That somehow somewhere down the line the error will sort itself out and they will not have wasted all of their effort and faith on the faulty teachings of a misled man.

The verse that should be kept in mind is 2 Peter 1:20, "Knowing this first, that no prophecy of the scripture is of any private interpretation" Time and time again Houteff interprets things in his own private way and then endeavors to convince others to see things the way he sees them. He laces together truths with error according to his misunderstanding of scripture not even maintaining harmony in his own theories, yet seeking to draw on Scripture and Ellen G. White to attempt to tie together the whole disastrous mess. His writings and his disciples continue to confuse and draw people away from the waymarks that have been the foundations of Adventist belief and he puts belief in his theories in the boat with other things pertaining to salvation, a value never ordained by God.

Ellen G. White says, "God has not passed His people by, and chosen one solitary man here another there as the only ones worthy to be entrusted with His truth. He does not give one man new light contrary to the established faith of the body. In every reform men have arisen making this claim. Paul warned the church in his day, 'Of your own selves shall men arise, speaking perverse things, to draw away disciples after them.' The greatest harm comes through those who go out from among them speaking perverse things. Through them the way of truth is evil spoken of. Let none be self confident, as though God has given them special light above their brethren. Christ is represented as dwelling in His people; and believers, as 'built upon the foundation of the apostles and prophets, Jesus Christ Himself being the chief cornerstone; in whom all the building, fitly framed together, growth unto a holy temple in the Lord; in whom ye also are builded together for a habitation of God through the Spirit." -*Counsels to Writers and Editors, pg. 45*.

"Satan hopes to involve the remnant people of God in the general ruin that is coming upon the earth. As the coming of Christ draws nigh, he will be more determined and decisive in his efforts to overthrow them. Men and women will arise professing to have some new light or some new revelation, whose tendency is to unsettle faith in the old landmarks. Their doctrines will not bear the test of God's word, yet souls will be deceived. False reports will be circulated, and some will be taken in this snare. They will believe these rumors, and in their turn will repeat them, and thus a link will be formed connecting them with the arch deceiver. This spirit will not always be manifested in an open defiance of the messages that God sends, but a settled unbelief is expressed in many ways. Every false statement that is made feeds and strengthens this unbelief, and through this means many souls will be balanced in the wrong direction. We cannot be too watchful against every form of error, for Satan is constantly seeking to draw men from the truth. He fills them with notions of their own sufficiency, and persuades them…that originality is a gift much to be coveted….One man has been drawn aside who is hard to be persuaded when once he has set his feet in a wrong track, and many who thought they were only following the man as he followed Christ are betrayed into following him when he has turned his back upon his Saviour."-*Testimonies for the Church, Vol. 5, pg. 296*.

The Bible says in Proverbs 14:12, "There is a way which seemeth right unto a man, but the end thereof are the ways of death." And in Proverbs 16:25, "There is a way that seemeth right unto a man, but the end thereof are the ways of death." In translation *that* and *which* are used, but in Hebrew the exact same words make up both verses. Solomon was the wisest man who ever lived and felt the need to say it twice. Many go out believing that they have truth. They "teach for doctrine the commandments of men." *Matthew 15:9 and Mark 7:7.* They forward their theories refusing to acknowledge the error within and teach others to be blind to it. They reject the argument because they have heard it before, not because the argument is faulty. They press forward with a message that fails to unite even them in its supposed truth, but insist on making the acceptance of it crucial to salvation. And to them it seems right, but the end thereof is death.

When I returned home from Tennessee I left everything behind. When I returned for my car, I was only able to bring back what would fit into a two door Nissan Sentra. I was homeless for a year and, though I tried, I was never able to return to recover the majority of what I left behind. Yet back at home, during that year, I experienced a peace I'd never known. Though I knew that returning to Tennessee would provide a place to lay my head, access to all of my possessions, and shelter for my child, I also knew that the road that led back to what I left in Tennessee was not the road that would end in Eternal life.

I can never say that I had riches like the young ruler portrayed in Scripture, but marriage, security, companionship, a father figure for my little one, were all my treasures. But Jesus said, "Yet lackest thou one thing: sell all that thou hast, and distribute unto the poor, and thou shalt have treasure in heaven: and come, follow me." In other words, "Give all you think you have up and follow Me. Stop heeding cunningly devised fables and seek first the Kingdom of God and His righteousness and all these treasures you think you currently possess, will actually, in their true form, be added unto you."

This, I did. I gave up my treasures and God gave me a home; an earthly one, along with the one He's preparing for me in heaven. He gave me security in that, "all things work together for good to them that love God, to them who are the called according to his purpose." *Romans 8:28.* He gave me companionship because, "thy Maker is thine husband; the LORD of hosts is his name; and thy Redeemer the Holy One of Israel; The God of the whole earth shall he be called." *Isaiah 54:5*. He provided a father figure for my little one in that He is "A father of the fatherless." *Psalm 68:5*. Everything that had stolen my peace He restored and it was by opening my eyes to the truth I already had, not manufacturing a new one.

As much as Saul and the others who believed as he did tried to show me the truth in Victor Houteff's writings, Houteff and God consistently showed me that the truth was not there to see and that I must be even more particular in my adherence to what is truth.

We must take seriously the instruction given in 2 Timothy 2: 15, "Study to shew thyself approved unto God, a workman that needeth not to be ashamed, rightly dividing the word of truth." Rightly dividing! *Orthotomeō!* To cut straight; to cut straight ways; to proceed on straight paths; hold a straight course; equivalent to doing right; to make straight and smooth; to handle aright; to teach the truth directly and correctly. Then, and only then, can we be safe from the many alterations Satan throws in our path. Then, and only then, can we differentiate between the Good Shepherd and a shepherd's fraud.

---

[1] *The version of events that took place in 1934 from the Denomination's view can be found at: www.shepherdsrod.com under the title, "The Story of the Shepherd's Rod". The version of events from Houteff's view can be found at: www.shepherds-rod-message.org under the title, "The Great Controversy Over the Shepherd's Rod".

[2] Name changed

www.ingramcontent.com/pod-product-compliance
Ingram Content Group UK Ltd.
Pitfield, Milton Keynes, MK11 3LW, UK
UKHW020239250726
13967UKWH00001B/461

9 780557 345984